HOW TO CONQUER Mental Mountains

BEYOND HABITS : PATH TO TRANSFORMATION

A BOOK BY

SB REYNOLD

BlueRose ONE.com
Stories Matter

BLUEROSE PUBLISHERS UK Ltd.
London

This book is primarily published and distributed in Great Britain and is also available in other global marketplaces.

ISBN: 978-93-6783-213-4

Designed and distributed by **BlueRoseONE.com** with global reach. Printing and fulfilment are managed through international distribution networks, ensuring availability based on order locations.

For publishing inquiries, visit **www.BlueRoseONE.com**

BlueRose Publishers UK Ltd,
Unit 3, 6-7 St Mary at Hill, London

+44 7386286323

First Edition: October 2025

Dedication

In dedication,

To my beloved parents, whose love, guidance and unwavering support has shaped me, and to my dear family and friends, whose encouragement and belief in me has carried me every step of the way.

Acknowledgement

To the Blue Rose Publishers team,

I would like to extend my heartfelt thanks to the entire editorial team at Blue Rose Publishers for their dedication, professionalism, and support in bringing this book to life. Your collaborative spirit and commitment have made this journey a truly rewarding experience. I am grateful for all the hard work and care you put into every step of the process.

Thank you for being wonderful partners in this endeavor.

Foreword

The most profound changes don't announce themselves—they unfold quietly through the choices we make when no one's watching. They arrive not with fanfare, but in the quiet moments—woven into the gentle rituals of morning, the thoughts we nurture, and the habits that shape our days without seeking recognition. True transformation is subtle, built on small, consistent decisions made long before anyone else notices.

This book is crafted as a companion for that kind of change.

Within these pages, you'll find grounded insights, timeless wisdom, and strategies to help you realign your daily actions with the person you aspire to become. You'll discover how early mornings can anchor your sense of purpose, how discipline can unlock true freedom, and how mentors—both present and unseen—leave lasting imprints on your journey. Through stories of healing, resilience, and growth, as well as case studies from some of today's most influential figures, this book offers a roadmap for meaningful, lasting transformation.

Each chapter is designed to help you reconnect with your inner rhythm, break free from limiting patterns, and find clarity amid life's chaos. Whether you're building new routines, mastering your focus, healing old wounds, or cultivating abundance, this journey is about growth that endures and peace that remains.

The wisdom you seek is already within you. This book simply offers a map to help you find your way back to it.

- Editor Blurrose Publishers

Disclaimer

All examples, experiences, and case studies presented in this book are intended solely for educational purposes and personal development. They are shared to inspire self-help and improvement.

Please note that the content provided does not constitute professional advice. Readers are strongly encouraged to consult with qualified professionals in the relevant fields before making any decisions based on the information in this book.

The author and publisher disclaim any liability arising directly or indirectly from the use of the material contained herein.

About the Author

Raised in a humble town in South Asia, S B Reynold grew up surrounded by the quiet strength and unwavering values of a close-knit family. With a father who dedicated his life to public service and a mother whose wisdom and warmth anchored the home, the foundation for a life built on integrity, empathy, and perseverance was laid early.

From an early age, S B Reynold understood the true meaning of sacrifice. His parents consistently placed the well-being and future of their children above their own comforts, instilling in him a sense of duty, discipline, and gratitude that would shape his life choices. Their lessons extended far beyond textbooks, they taught him humility, respect, and how to stay grounded no matter where life took him.

Fueled by this upbringing, S B Reynold pursued academic excellence, completing a Master's in Information Systems and later undertaking business executive education at the esteemed Cambridge Judge Business School. These milestones were not achieved alone. The unyielding support of his family, extended relatives, and close friends served as the backbone of his journey, a network of encouragement that carried him through both triumphs and trials.

Professionally, the author has held leadership roles in top multinational software corporations, collaborating with clients across the UK, Australia, Germany, and beyond. His cross-cultural experiences and people-first approach to leadership reflect the values he was raised with- respect, resilience, and responsibility.

This book is born from the belief that success is not reserved for a select few. If he could overcome doubt, obstacles, and limitations, so can you. It's not about shortcuts or privilege, it's about showing up, every day, and doing the work. His story is not one of overnight success, but of steady persistence and an unshakable mindset.

Through his writing, S. B. Reynold hopes to pay tribute to his parents, the true heroes of his journey, and to inspire others to believe in their own potential. Because at the heart of it all, he believes one thing deeply:

If he can do it, so can you.

In essence, He is deeply passionate about this book because he believes it has the power to positively impact and enrich people's lives. Drawing from his own experiences, he aims to share insights and practical guidance that can inspire growth, resilience, and meaningful change. Through his work, he hopes to empower others to navigate their transformation journeys with confidence and purpose.

Introduction

If you are reading this page, there must have been a reason for doing so in this given instance. Perhaps a calling of sorts, something that compelled you to read this book amidst many other genres and subjects. I am a firm believer in the philosophy that everything in the universe follows a pattern and we happen to form a speck in a magnanimous collaboration of the cosmos. "Moving forward with this line of thought, if you decided to read this book:" based on the **title, "How to Conquer Mental Mountains – Beyond Habits: Path to Transformation"**

Whether you're someone actively seeking personal transformation—breaking free from vices, shedding outdated habits, or simply striving for a better version of yourself—or just a curious traveler flipping through these pages during a long-haul flight or a quiet coffee break, this book is for you. It's not just about changing habits; it's about transcending them. It's about understanding the deeper layers of your mind, confronting the invisible barriers that hold you back, and discovering the path to lasting change.

Either way, all readers are much welcome, the book is structured to be of benefit to all categories of readers, and hopefully, by the end of the read, you can expect a shift in perspective that could go on to act as a catalyst in shaping your life in a way you have always desired. The book acts as a cohesive compilation of some of the most tried, tested, and verified hacks for becoming the ultimate self-actualized version of yourself. Besides being a self-help book as one may deduce based on the cover page, I have attempted to create a book that seeks to inspire and ignite the ultimate version of you that is yet to see the light of the day, as you go ahead with each chapter, I hope that the knowledge you gain through every insight peels off your layers, like the multitude layers of skin of an onion, one by one, taking away the facades of societal pressures, insecurities, inhibitions and much darker and deeply compressed parts of your consciousness.

An overtly thought rhetorical question, which one might have pondered upon at least once in their lives, even fleetingly, is "What sets us apart from those who have accomplished greatness in life?", "What is something they have that I don't" the question in itself is flawed in its essence, because the right question would be something along the lines of, "What are they doing right, which I am not?" because as humans we all are much more similar to one another than we would like to believe, our capabilities and capacities have very negligible differences if we look at it comprehensively at a larger scheme. We are all born with the same innate potential as one another, the only thing that distinguishes us from those who have attained success and maximized their potential is their habits and rituals. These attributes can greatly influence where you stand in the race of life.

The achievers live their lives in a specifically designed manner, they are the owners of their destiny. Once you reclaim power and autonomy over your life, you can design your life in whichever way you deem fit, you would be free to head in limitless directions and live the life of champions. The extraordinary are set apart from the ordinary in their daily habits and routines. Every moment of your day has the capacity to shape your life in a significant manner, the small things add up to a bigger moment, like a butterfly effect; a concept from chaos theory that suggests small, seemingly insignificant actions can lead to huge, unpredictable outcomes. It's famously illustrated by the idea that the flap of a butterfly's wings in Brazil could trigger a tornado in Texas. The term was coined by meteorologist Edward Lorenz, who discovered that tiny changes in initial conditions could drastically alter weather predictions. This idea shows how complex systems, like weather or even human decisions, are sensitive to small changes.

If you are reading this page, you probably are one of the few people who have an inner voice calling out to you, pushing you to fulfill your potential and embody your highest self. Very few people in life get to have the privilege of waking up one day and feeling an innate urge to do something bigger, something better, like a voice calling out to you from the depths of your inner consciousness, asking for more, a strong feeling that you were meant to do something profound. When you have that recurring thought, sit with it and stick to it. Carry it with you on your difficult days and on the days you feel accomplished. Know that the voice exists for a reason, It is a force pushing you to do something you were born for. Honour and celebrate that voice through conscious actions and beneficial habits. On believing your intuition and sticking to your dreams, and acting towards them, you would be astounded to see the changes in your life within a year.

The how-to's will be covered intensively in the chapters, from waking up to the energized and recalibrated air of the dawn to the priceless knowledge about the art of transforming ideas to execution, with added emphasis on acing the execution part, the book acts as a catalyst, a guide and a pandora's box of secrets to unearth the highest self.

There is an abundance of self-help books that attempt to help you with the same, however, this book blends some of my life experiences, and ideas from some of the most prolific thinkers and achievers of our time, and acts as a compilation of all the best systems the world has come up with to aid one achieve self actualization. This read hopefully provides you with a holistic perspective on what it takes to get on top.

With case studies of personalities, substantially researched data to support your journey, and exclusive anecdotes from my personal experience as someone who has come a long way from my humble beginnings, the book provides an overview of what it is like, to live the life of your dreams, to navigate tough circumstances and to cross the bridge of limitations, hurdles and habits that tie you down and getting to the greener side. The book also contains a summary at the end of each chapter, for those individuals in a rush or for those who need a brief refresh of the material after finishing the book.

Wishing all the dear readers a happy read, may you accomplish everything you have ever dreamt of.

Contents

Chapter 1:

Early Morning Routine: Syncing with Circadian Rhythm

The earth rotates along its axis, giving us dusk and dawn, the light and the dark. The Egyptians created the 24-hour widely accepted time division based on the light of the day and the darkness of night, long before astronomy paved the way for creating standardized and structured time divisions. Our ancestors were habituated to waking up to the sounds of nature rewiring itself to set forth on a new day, a fresh beginning, with the birds chirping, humming of bees and the dew drops splattering on the ground with soft rays of the magnanimous sun gently caressing the foliage and its inhabitants, sending a viscerally invigorating message, that a new day has begun.

Today, In the life of us civilized and urbanized homo sapiens, mornings look vastly different. The morning is a cumbersome ritual that repeats day after day, symbolizing a new day of just getting by and making it through. Some youth wake up groggy after a late night out partying or doom-scrolling on social media, while others are up late working or studying. Both ends of the spectrum dread waking up with the sunrise, thanks to their compromised sleep hours. And there is another peculiar group of individuals, albeit less in number, who wake up before the dawn begins, they are ready to step out of their homes at the same time the sun is awoken from its slumber. The contrast is damning, how can we as common species be so different in behavior? especially one that is deeply encoded in our primitive instincts.

A lot of factors play into why you would say something like, "I'm not a morning person!'. The average amount of sleep an adult body requires is about 7 hours per day, any drastic difference in the margin is a disaster waiting to happen for the rest of the day ahead. Your sleep quality also affects how enthusiastic you are about waking up to a fresh start. When we talk about today's sleep-related behaviors, we cannot leave out the inevitable and most cliche-sounding term, 'lifestyle changes" It probably has to be one of the most overused terms while talking about forming healthy lifestyles and routines, but it is overused for a very factual reason.

During the Anthropocene, we saw a revolution that would soon cause a massive upheaval in the functioning of previously known human societies, it was the Industrial Revolution, that brought us some of the most irreplaceable technologies that shifted the trajectory of humanity. With the introduction of convenient transport, mechanical machinery, and of the most important inventions, the light bulb! By manifesting the light into our lives through artificial means, we could decide when it was day and when it was night for us within our four-walled enclosures. However, our primitive part of the brain which controls the secretion of a hormone called melatonin, which makes us sleepy, cannot distinguish between artificial light and natural sunlight. So by exposing ourselves to white light and blue light after sunset, we can inhibit melatonin production which can get us to stay up late.

These factors in combination with poor diet, stress, and exercise, can cause damage to our body's natural circadian rhythm, which is the body's naturally occurring 24-hour clock in sync with dusk and dawn. It regulates some of the key primary human functions, such as sleep, hormone release, appetite, digestion, and temperature. It is operated based on visual cues, which are, sunlight and darkness, but, lately with an increase in artificial light sources in the surroundings, the circadian rhythm of the body is paying the price. Caffeine is a powerful chemical when consumed as per the circadian rhythm to support the body's function, it can have beneficial manifestations, on the other hand, the use of coffee or caffeinated beverages after the sun sets can derail the natural 24-hour biological clock, leading to hormonal dysfunctions, which further escalated to some of the chronic lifestyle originating diseases.

It might seem challenging to shift your sleep cycle to a much more beneficial one, but doing so can bring about positive changes in your physiology, mental health, and overall well-being.

Now that we have delved into why it is important to have a proper sleep schedule, we can also learn about why it is important to wake up early in the morning (finally coming down to the theme of the chapter!)

Waking up early in the morning is not just a habit; it's a powerful tool for syncing with your body's natural rhythm and unlocking a range of benefits. Biologically, Many studies have time and again demonstrated that people who wake earlier are less likely to develop depression, anxiety, or other mood disorders, thanks to proper hormonal regulation. Those who wake up earlier also tend to eat food earlier, thus preventing blood sugar levels from crashing and insulin regulation. They are also exposed to morning sunlight which works wonders on mental health and the production of Dopamine, which is a mood-boosting chemical. Waking up early aligns with your body's natural biological clock, fueling your energy levels in a way that is far more invigorating than staying up late and disrupting your sleep cycle. By greeting the day with the sun, you tap into a natural surge of alertness and agility, making it easier to feel sharp and focused throughout the day.

On a mental and mindset scale, One of the most noticeable perks is the mental boost it provides. Imagine this: as you rise from bed, despite your mind's resistance to leaving the comfort of slumber, you're already taking charge. That simple act of overcoming your desire to stay cozy can create a sense of accomplishment, setting a positive tone for the entire day. Compare that to the grogginess of oversleeping, when your body feels out of sync and your mind sluggish, it's clear why starting early can leave you feeling more fulfilled.

Incorporating this habit into your routine doesn't just improve your mornings, it can transform your entire life. With regulated hormones and a body that feels energized and in tune with its natural rhythm, you'll notice an increase in productivity, motivation, and overall happiness. It's amazing how waking up early can unlock your full potential, setting the stage for a day filled with vigor and success.

Mornings are an optimal time to fulfill daunting tasks which include tasks that involve physical movement, creativity, spirituality, and skill development. The dawn is the time when your body and mind feel fresh, it's best to kickstart the day with a routine that can help you become the best version of yourself. By incorporating practices or rituals daily, even for a short period in the morning, you can achieve great feats and see humongous differences in yourself within a short span of time.

One of the most daunting challenges of the present day lifestyle happens to be our sedentary routine. From school to workspace, we are often required to sit still and stay seated for hours extending the optimal amount. To counter the inevitable lifestyle changes,, regular physical exercise is a non negotiable, exercise in the morning is deemed to be more beneficial when compared to exercise in any other time of the day from a psychological perspective, since the physiological effects tend to remain constant whichever time of the day you choose to workout, according to several studies. Exercise aids in reduction of cortisol; the stress hormone, boosts metabolism, and is seen to have an inverse effect on cardiovascular risks. In addition, morning workouts have been observed to increase strength and reduced recovery time post an intense training session.

The psychological benefits of regular morning exercise are of immense significance, as research findings demonstrate that those who workout in the mornings are seen to incorporate a healthy lifestyle through the rest of the day, they are also prone to making healthier diet choices amongst several other mental health benefits.

Another important component of a morning routine is breakfast, the king of all meals. It is said to be the most important meal of the day, for very valid reasons. Regular intake of a well balanced breakfast improves glycemic control and reduces the risk of cardiovascular diseases. Eating a big meal in the morning, and reduced snacking has shown to reduce BMI in overweight individuals, with a remarkable significance in fat loss. A complete, nutritious breakfast, rich in protein, fiber, carbs and healthy fats satiates us throughout the day, leading to reduced bingeing of processed or not-so-healthy food choices. Especially in the youth and adolescents, breakfast plays a huge role in cognitive development.

In the summer of 2021, while I was browsing through a book store on a very spontaneous stroll across my neighbourhood in West London, I came across a book titled *The 5 AM Club.* The story revolves around the transformative journey of two individuals; A man and a woman, the former an artist grappling with creative block and the latter an entrepreneur going through difficulties in her business, who are introduced to a life-changing philosophy by a charismatic mentor named Riley. He takes them to Mauritius, where they meet the Spellbinder, a wise figure who guides them through a profound process of self-discovery. Their experience in Mauritius becomes a pivotal chapter in their lives, helping them cultivate new habits and establish a powerful morning routine that ultimately leads to personal growth and success. The book, called the " 5 AM club", by Robin Sharma, gives an extensive overview of the importance of a morning routine and introduces a concept called the 20-20-20 formula, which I am going to explain very briefly. Here a very interesting hack is formulated, that can aid in setting up a very beneficial routine, even for the busy-bees! All it takes is one hour or 60 minutes. He asks you to divide those 60 minutes into three parts, 20 minutes each.

The First 20 Minutes: Movement and Awakening the Body

The alarm rings, and the world is still asleep. But you, you're up. You've decided to take control of this day, and your first step is clear: move. Sharma calls this the "20-minute burst" that awakens your body and ignites your inner vitality. This is not just about physical exercise, it's a deliberate effort to activate every cell in your body, to flood your system with energy, and to jump-start your day in the best possible way. Physical movement is the key to unlocking your energy. It's like the ignition of a powerful engine. It wakes up your muscles, sharpens your focus, and floods your bloodstream with a rush of endorphins; the body's natural mood elevators. Whether it's a brisk jog, a set of push-ups, or a series of stretches, the point is to get your heart pumping, your body moving, and your spirit energized. Exercise doesn't just make your body stronger, it strengthens your mind. By the end of these 20 minutes, you'll feel more awake, more alive, and more prepared to tackle the challenges that lie ahead. You're setting the stage for a day filled with strength, resilience, and clarity.

The Second 20 Minutes: Reflecting and Awakening the Mind

Usually, one of the biggest contributors to poor sleep quality is stress, the added burden of the previous day is carried over to the next day. How can you reset your mind and hit the refresh button? Once your body is awake, it's time to turn inward. The second section of the formula is all about reflection, a dedicated 20-minute period for silence, mindfulness, and connection to your higher self. This is your time to center your thoughts, calm your mind, and create a mental space that supports your growth and success. No more distractions. No more noise. Just you, your thoughts, and your intentions. Take a deep breath. Reflect.

Sharma suggests three powerful ways to enhance mindfulness, these are; meditation, journaling, and visualization. These methods will be discussed extensively in the coming chapters. The goal here is to calm the noise of the outside world and engage deeply with the inner world. In this sacred 20 minutes, you're cultivating mindfulness, sharpening your focus, and setting yourself up for a day filled with purpose. The benefit? A focused mind that's clear, centered, and ready to handle whatever comes your way.

The Third 20 Minutes: Growing and Awakening the Soul

With your body moving and your mind focused, it's time to grow. The final 20 minutes of your hour are dedicated to learning, self-improvement, and nourishing your soul. This is where you invest in your future, where you engage in activities that fuel your growth and take your life to the next level. Sharma emphasizes that the pursuit of growth is a lifelong journey. And what better way to start than with 20 minutes of intentional learning every single morning? How you choose to grow is up to you, but here are some ideas:

1. Reading: Whether it's a powerful book on personal development, a biography of someone who inspires you, or a piece of fiction that sparks your creativity, reading is one of the best ways to expand your mind. Aim for at least 10–15 pages in the morning, and you'll be amazed at how quickly you absorb new insights.

2. Podcasts or Audiobooks: If you're on the go, you can listen to educational podcasts or audiobooks. These can be on a variety of topics- business, philosophy, psychology, history, or even health and wellness. The idea is to expose yourself to new ideas and wisdom that expand your worldview.

3. Skill Development: Invest in learning a new skill. Whether it's coding, photography, public speaking, or even learning a new language, the process of continuous learning keeps your brain sharp and adaptable.

This time is not about mindless consumption, it's about intentional, purposeful growth. You're feeding your mind with knowledge that will serve you not just today, but for the rest of your life.The reward? A soul that's ever-evolving, a life that's always progressing, and a mindset that thrives on learning and improvement.

By the time your first hour has passed, you've given your body, mind, and soul everything they need to thrive. This is not just a morning routine. This is a blueprint for life optimization. The 20-20-20 formula doesn't just help you "survive" the day. It helps you thrive. It ensures that every day, you're physically energized, mentally clear, and continuously growing into the best version of yourself. The secret, according to Sharma, is simple: Master the first hour of your day, and you master your life. So, tomorrow morning, when the alarm rings, you have a choice: you can hit snooze, or you can step into the 5 AM Club and begin your day with purpose, energy, and growth. The choice is yours. And remember, your future self will thank you for the decision you make today.

Every action you take today can have an exponential benefit by the end of the year, or even in a couple of months, it is important to note that it is a series of small actions every day that can bring about a drastic change in your life, scattered days of intensive work are unsustainable long term and can lead to frustration and burn out because of inconsistent or slow results. With small efforts, consistently throughout a period of time, you are bound to see consistent, faster and long-term results.

Waking up is one such habit that the most successful people around us incorporate into their lives, I personally have seen a tremendous shift in my productivity and mental health once I started waking up early and began incorporating a morning routine in the first hour of waking up. Why is it a winner's habit? It is the habit of champions because waking up before the dawn or along with it, sets you ahead of millions of others who don't. You have a couple hours of headstart to the day in contrast to those who sleep in late. The headstart might seem insignificant because at the end of the day, we all have 24 hours right? So what makes the early birds special? The early morning hours give us time to work on ourselves with a fresh mind and body, in comparison to late night hours when we are drained by other aspects of life such as work, education, and family responsibilities. An individual who is keen on working on oneself would be more productive in one routine if they started them in the morning, before other responsibilities took over, in sharp difference to trying to work out or read a book or gain some new skill at the end of the day where our energy resources are at the bottom of the tank and when the brain is at the brink of exhaustion.

It is also equally important to set up a productive morning routine once you have gotten accustomed to rising with the sun. A routine structures a map to your goal, it is the catalyst that will bring about lasting changes. When you wake up early in the morning, it is pertinent to leverage your body's peak mental and physical performance in building goal-oriented and developmental morning routines. In her book, *What the Most Successful People Do Before Breakfast*, Laura Vanderkam talks in depth about what sets successful individuals apart, when it comes to structuring their morning routines. Let's explore some of the key takeaways from her outstanding book and build up on our "how to?" when we have just covered the "when to?".

During the shrill London winter of 2021, I came across a particular book which I found truly inspiring and interesting. As I indulged in my daily cup of coffee, a few flips of the pages turned into a dedicated read of the book, unexpectedly, it was perhaps one of the finest reads of that year. I integrated many of its insights into my own life, consciously, and subconsciously and keenly enough, they've had a significant impact. Here are some key takeaways that I believe could help you on your journey to self-improvement and enhancing productivity. In her magnum opus of a book *What the Most Successful People Do Before Breakfast*, Laura Vanderkam explores how high achievers structure their mornings to set themselves up for success. Drawing on interviews and research, she reveals that successful people don't just wake up early- they use the first hours of their day with intention and purpose. Here are some key pointers:

Vanderkam argues that how successful people spend their morning hours before the typical workday begins is crucial. These individuals tend to wake up early, often before the world is awake, to focus on personal growth, health, and productivity. The time before breakfast is a period of self-care, planning, and skill-building that prepares them to tackle the day's challenges with energy and focus.

Successful people often have well-established morning routines. These routines can vary but typically include activities like:

Exercise: Many top performers use the morning for physical activity, whether it is running, yoga, or a gym session. This boosts their energy and helps them clear their minds.

Planning the Day: Successful individuals often take time to plan their day, prioritize their goals, and set intentions. This helps them manage their time more effectively and stay on track.

Personal Development: Reading, writing, and learning something new are often key components of their mornings. These activities help them grow and stay sharp both personally and professionally.

One of the main insights from Vanderkam's research is that the most successful people don't wait for the perfect moment to focus on personal goals. Instead, they deliberately carve out time in the early hours of the day. By waking up earlier, they gain extra time to focus on priorities that might otherwise be sidelined by work or other commitments.

Vanderkam also emphasizes the importance of getting enough sleep, despite the focus on early mornings. She argues that the most successful people recognize the importance of rest and balance their morning productivity with healthy sleep habits.

Vanderkam's research suggests that successful people don't simply make time for work- they make time for their personal lives, family, and passions. The key is to be intentional with how they use their time, especially before breakfast. This deliberate focus on what truly matters helps them achieve balance, reduce stress, and stay fulfilled.

A central concept in Vanderkam's work is the idea of a "168-hour week"- the total number of hours in a week. By breaking the day into smaller segments, successful people can align their time with their long-term goals. Morning routines are a critical part of this strategy, as they allow individuals to start the day with focus and purpose, aligning their activities with their overarching goals.

There also has been a few notable studies which indicate a shift in the brain chemistry of individuals who wake up early. Early risers often have more consistent sleep patterns and may experience better quality sleep. Research has shown that sufficient and high-quality sleep is crucial for cognitive functions such as memory, problem-solving, and emotional regulation. These are crucial cognitive functions that can help us achieve our goals efficiently.

Waking up early might have seemed redundant when you first started the chapter. Hopefully, by the end of it, you will be more informed about the perks of a morning routine and rising with the dawn. To get to the version of yourself that you aspire the most, it is inevitable to bring about positive changes in lifestyle and yourself, one of the routines that can kickstart your self development journey could be the simple habit of waking up early. They don't say "the early bird catches the worm"for no reason!

Key notes from the chapter-

1. Syncing with the Circadian Rhythm: Our bodies are naturally programmed to follow the 24-hour cycle of light and dark. Disrupting this rhythm with artificial light, poor sleep, and unhealthy habits impacts our physical and mental well-being. Aligning with this rhythm by waking up early can enhance sleep quality, hormone regulation, and energy levels.
2. Benefits of Waking Up Early: Early risers experience improved mental health, sharper focus, better mood regulation, and enhanced productivity. Exposure to morning sunlight boosts dopamine levels, and nutritious breakfast within two hours of waking up helps with better blood sugar and insulin management.
3. Health Benefits of Exercise and Breakfast: Morning exercise reduces stress, boosts metabolism, and fosters long-term healthy habits. A nutritious breakfast improves glycemic control, reduces cravings, and fuels both the body and mind for the day ahead.
4. The 20-20-20 Formula (Robin Sharma's "5 AM Club"):
   - First 20 minutes: Exercise to awaken the body, boost endorphins, and ignite energy.
   - Next 20 minutes: Reflect through mindfulness, journaling, or meditation to center your thoughts and reset your mind.
   - Last 20 minutes: Grow through learning, reading, or skill-building to nurture personal development.
5. Morning Routines Drive Success: Successful people leverage the early hours for personal growth, planning, and health. According to Laura Vanderkam's research, this includes exercising, setting goals for the day, and

prioritizing personal development before daily responsibilities take over.

6. Small Daily Actions Lead to Big Results: Consistently waking up early and building an intentional morning routine creates exponential benefits over time. Starting the day with focus and purpose, rather than chaos or sluggishness, fosters long-term productivity, mental clarity, and life satisfaction.

Chapter 2:
The Art of Borrowing Wisdom from Mentors.

"The delicate balance of mentoring someone is not creating them in your own image but giving them the opportunity to create themselves." - Steven Spielberg

The book talks about transformation and self-actualization, so why is there an entire chapter on mentors you might wonder? In recent times we are witnesses to a fairly new phenomenon, one that is called individualism. However, since our birth to our imminent death, we are circumnavigating in a loop of learning and unlearning, socializing in a complexly weaved network of various subsystems which carefully intertwine to form a larger system. We are introduced to language, culture, society and other functions of existence through individuals who are experienced and superior to us in terms of skills and knowledge, it could be anyone, from your parents, to your boss at work.

From the times I learnt my first alphabets with my mother guiding my hand which clutched onto the pencil to form legible symbols on the notebook, to the times I strutted down the school hallway with a bag half my size, greeted by the warm gaze of my patient teacher, to my early days in the corporate trying to find my place amongst colleagues and bosses, and on my visits to bengaluru on my breaks where I remember meeting my cousin who was a software professional, who also happened to inspire me immensely because of whom I have built a successful career in the same field, I remember always having someone to look up to, a sort of guiding figure. My social circle expanded, from family, friends to colleagues, and in each group I found a particular set of people who have had a tremendous influence in shaping my identity.

An individual is a sum of collective experiences, and a huge part of our experiences are comprised of our interaction with other people, from our behavior, to our core identity, we are shaped by the opinions of those around us, to a larger extent than we would like to believe. When we are growing up, we have a set of individuals who play an impeccable role in our growth and development, be it physical, mental or social. Our parents nurture us with nutrition, shelter, and most importantly, love, they are our first link to the wider network of kinships and society. When we are admitted to schools, our teachers take over, followed by lecturers and professors as our education progresses, and eventually, we join a workforce, where mentors guide us. In fact, learning is such a huge component in life, that we have these guiding figures even in other aspects of our life, be it spirituality, health, romantic relationships, and innumerable other fragments of life.

The relationship between two individuals, who share a bond of a mentor and mentee is defined as a professional, working alliance in which individuals work together over time to support the personal and professional growth, development, and success of the relational partners through the provision of career and psychosocial support. The relationship is distinguishable from the relationship of a student and teacher, based on the inclusion of mental and emotional support as well, this bond requires building rapport between the two parties and is often a personal bond that involves mutual understanding and collaboration.

Mentorship and learning come in myriad forms, sometimes the relationship of mentor-mentee is clearly defined between both parties, and sometimes they take more of a covert form with either one or both parties unaware of the larger implications and influence they might have over one another.

The reason we need mentors in life is because on our path to self-actualization, we get a chance to avoid making the same mistakes our predecessors have made, we can get a nuanced perspective on the path we are setting forth on, and be well equipped to face any hindrance or limitations that might come our way. To become the best version of oneself, one must not only go through a series of trials and errors but also pick the smarter way of choosing the right things at the right time. Mentors act as catalysts and guiding lights toward our goal, which aids us in reaching our potential faster and easier.

The mentor.

A mentor is an experienced and trusted advisor who provides guidance, support, and wisdom to help someone grow personally or professionally.

They are guides, catalysts, and nurturers of potential. They offer wisdom from experience to help a mentee navigate challenges and avoid mistakes. They instill confidence, inspire growth, and provide support, pushing the mentee beyond perceived limits. They share knowledge, offer feedback, and encourage development, helping their mentee navigate challenges and make informed decisions.

A mentor also happens to be an individual who might sometimes see in you the potential that might have previously been unnoticed by you and those around you, it takes a special person to see the greatness and capability within you and try to work together in bringing it out in its purest and most powerful form into whichever avenue you're pursuing.

The best example of this would be one of the world's fastest humans, Usain Bolt, and his coach, Glen Mills story, initially a 200m specialist, Bolt soon switched to the 100m track with the help of Glen, with whose guidance he went on to create the world record of 9.58 seconds in 2009, at the berlin world championships in Germany. When Bolt joined Mills in 2004, he was a raw talent with a love for speed but a disdain for training and discipline. Mills saw what others didn't: a once-in-a-lifetime athlete who just happened to need the right guidance. He fixed Bolt's sluggish starts, refined his stride, and built his endurance, all while transforming his mindset from a laid-back prodigy to a relentless competitor.

The mentee.

However, the Mentor-Mentee relationship goes both ways, you cannot expect to land a Glen Mills in your life without having the courage, aptitude, and drive of a seeker willing to do everything it takes to fulfill their goal.

True wisdom is gained not only through personal experiences but also by absorbing the insights of those who have walked the path before us. A mentor serves as a guiding light, illuminating the road ahead so that the mentee does not stumble where others have. However, the true essence of learning lies not just in the mentor's wisdom but also in the mentee's willingness to observe, listen, and internalize.

A mentee must first observe keenly, not just what is taught explicitly but also the actions, habits, and silent lessons that a mentor demonstrates. Every decision, every strategy, and even the demeanor of a mentor holds valuable insights. By watching with intent, a mentee can decode the unspoken wisdom embedded in experience.

Beyond observation, a mentee must listen with both ears and an open mind. A great mentor does not merely instruct; they share lessons carved out of their own triumphs and failures. Every word, every piece of advice, carries years of distilled experience, a shortcut to wisdom that the mentee may otherwise take decades to uncover. Active listening fosters not just knowledge but also understanding the bridge between knowing and applying.

Yet, learning does not stop at hearing and seeing; the most crucial step is imbibing and applying these lessons. Knowledge without action is like a lamp left unlit. A mentee must internalize the teachings, adapt them to their journey, and act upon them with conviction. This conscious effort to integrate wisdom into one's actions is what helps avoid unnecessary hardships and mistakes.

A successful mentor-mentee relationship is not a passive exchange but a dynamic process, one where the mentee is not just a receiver but an active participant in their own growth. By watching, listening, and applying, the mentee honors the wisdom of the mentor and transforms it into a legacy of success.

A spectacular example of a learner and a mentee would be Eklavya, a character from the Hindu Epic, Mahabharata. When Eklavya pursued Dronacharya, a master of warfare, who was a teacher of the Pandavas and Kauravas, to teach him archery, Dronacharya dismissed the poor boy because of his humble lineage which was contrary to the royal heirs he predominantly mentored. Despite the rejection, a determined Eklavya sought to learn from the renowned master by keenly observing his techniques from a distance. Eklavya mimicked and practiced tirelessly, refining his archery skills through self-discipline and perseverance. His unwavering belief in Drona's teachings, even without direct mentorship, allowed him to surpass many trained warriors. However, the relationship ended in tragedy after Drona discovered Eklavya's practice of taking lessons from him covertly. The tale, however, stands as a lasting testimony to the sheer dedication and will of Eklavya, who demonstrates the virtues of a model mentee.

A triumphant collaboration between mentor and mentees.

In my personal experience in the corporate world, I have had the pleasure of witnessing complex ideas and ambitions come to fruition after a successful collaboration of team members, where more than often, someone assumes the role of mentor and the other of a mentee. Teamwork drives the basis of success in any corporate setup. In my opinion, it is in everyone's interest if every team member is fully aware of their shortcomings and strengths, this aids in reaching out to those who are more capable than us in particular facets which in turn helps bring our productive results. Two astounding cases come to my mind when I think of workspace mentorships, one of google and the other of Apple inc, both large global conglomerates that are expanding and growing at an exponential rate.

Every once in a while I recollect a beautiful example of a corporate mentor-mentee relationship that turned into a groundbreaking collaborative effort that revolutionized the IT industry.

The partnership between Sergey Brin, Larry Page, and Eric Schmidt is a fascinating case of corporate leadership and mentorship, showcasing how a blend of visionary founders and an experienced executive can shape a global empire. Their relationship at Google highlights the power of mentorship in leadership, decision-making, and business growth.

The story begins In 1998, when Stanford PhD students, Larry page and Sergey Brin co-founded Google, introducing groundbreaking ideas in search algorithms and digital innovation. However, their expertise fell short when it came to the corporate experience needed to scale their innovation into a global business.

In 2001, venture capitalist John Doerr who happened to be one of Google's investors encouraged Brin and Page to bring in experienced leadership to manage the rapidly growing company. The initially hesitant duo appointed Eric Schmidt, former CEO of Novell and Sun microsystems and a respected computer scientist, as Google's CEO. Page and Brin accepted Schmidt as their mentor in corporate leadership, allowing Google to transition from a startup into a structured, high-growth company.

This collaboration led to a powerful dynamic between the trio, Eric Schmidt served as a mentor, providing strategic leadership that guided Google through business expansion, partnerships, and IPO readiness. Meanwhile, Larry Page and Sergey Brin focused on technology, product development, and vision, ensuring Google stayed at the cutting edge. Their relationship fostered mutual learning, as Schmidt adapted to Google's fast-moving, unconventional culture, while Page and Brin absorbed crucial lessons in scaling, operations, and executive decision-making.

By 2011, the mentor had done his job, and it was time for the protégés to take the reins. Larry Page stepped in as CEO, while Schmidt transitioned into the role of Executive Chairman, a move that signified a changing of the guard. No longer the wide-eyed innovators of their Stanford days,

Page and Brin had evolved into seasoned leaders, ready to shape the future of Google and its ever-expanding empire. Their leadership would soon extend beyond search engines, driving the formation of Alphabet Inc., a bold restructuring that cemented their legacy as pioneers of the digital age.

Some of the key leadership and mentorship lesson takeaways from this particular case include-

- Vision needs experience- in corporate settings, especially startups and freshly started ventures, innovation and vision are abundant, however, it takes a seasoned mentor to guide the team toward long-term and sustainable success. Founders benefit from seasoned mentors to navigate corporate complexities.
- A good mentor enables, not controls- if a mentor needs to impose a particular task or learning onto a mentee, it stops being a mentor-mentee relationship and turns into a teacher-student relationship. The basis of mentorship revolves around collaboration and cooperation, the aim is to guide, nurture, and aid in the creation of something bigger than both parties involved.
- Growth requires transition- A mentor-mentee relationship cannot last forever, because the aim is to equip the mentee with skills and knowledge so they can pave the way for their success. Effective mentorship prepares mentees to eventually lead on their own.

The Brin-Page-Schmidt dynamic is a brilliant textbook example of how mentorship in corporate leadership fosters innovation, stability, and long-term success.

In your corporate or work setting, it also becomes really important to retain your authenticity and stay true to your core values. An invaluable trait a mentee can have is one of discernment. A mentor comes with their own set of beliefs and experiences that can often create a bias in the output they provide. At times, having the skill to discern between useful and redundant guidance is key to making the path to success your own. This again is illustrated with a larger-than-life example of Satya Nadella and his mentor at Microsoft, Steve Ballmer.

Steve Ballmer ran Microsoft like a high-energy sales juggernaut; Shouting, sweating, and pushing Windows everywhere. He mentored Satya Nadella, recognizing his tech genius and putting him in charge of Azure, Microsoft's cloud future. But when Nadella took over as CEO in 2014, he didn't just tweak the blueprint, he tossed it out!

Gone were the hard-hitting, market-dominating battles. Instead, Nadella embraced collaboration, cloud computing, AI, and even partnerships with old rivals. He transformed Microsoft from a Windows-obsessed giant into a cloud-first, AI-driven powerhouse.

While Ballmer was Nadella's mentor in a corporate sense, Nadella took Microsoft in a dramatically different direction, showcasing how mentees can learn from their predecessors while redefining their own path.

In other scenarios, the contrasting energies between the mentor and mentee can often create a collaborative dreamwork. It creates an alchemy of sorts that just seems to work out effortlessly. Such was the case of Steve Jobs and Tim Cook, the pioneers of Apple Inc.

Steve Jobs was the big-picture genius, the relentless perfectionist who made technology feel like magic. Tim Cook? He was the master strategist, the behind-the-scenes force who made sure Apple's operations ran like a Swiss watch. Their mentor-mentee relationship wasn't built on similarities, it was built on balance.

Jobs brought Cook on board in 1998, not to dream up the next iPhone, but to fix Apple's messy supply chain. And Cook delivered- he slashed costs, streamlined production, and built a global logistics empire, ensuring Apple could deliver products at an unmatched scale. Jobs focused on creating the future, while Cook made sure the future arrived on time.

As Jobs' health declined, he knew Apple needed stability, not another visionary, so he handpicked Cook as his successor in 2011. Many doubted Cook, he wasn't a showman, he wasn't a product guy. But he played to his strengths, transforming Apple into a $3 trillion juggernaut by expanding services (Apple Music, iCloud), wearables (Apple Watch, AirPods), and hardware independence (Apple Silicon).

The lesson? Great mentees don't replace their mentors, they evolve the vision.

It is not only in our career and education that we find a need for a mentor, there are multitude of other aspects of life where mentorship and guidance is key to fulfilling one's goals. One could seek spiritual guidance, financial, emotional or mental guidance from a mentor.

The divine mentor from the Geeta.

On the battlefield of Kurukshetra, as the war drenched the soil red like the colour of the setting sun covered the sky, as fate was destined to unfurl, A perplexed Arjuna turned to Krishna, his charioteer, mentor, and divine guide. Overwhelmed by doubt, he confessed:

"Krishna, I can stop the wind with my hands, but how do I control my restless mind?"

Krishna, ever calm, smiled and replied:

"Through practice and detachment, O Arjuna."

Arjuna's struggle wasn't against enemies alone, it was against his own wavering mind, fears, and attachments. The mind, like the wind, is ever-moving, unpredictable, and untamed. Yet, Krishna's wisdom held the key: discipline (Abhyasa) and detachment (Vairagya).

This snippet out of the all time favourite epic of Mine, the Bhagavad geeta, talks about how even the mightiest of warriors, Arjuna, had his moments of doubt and confusion, only to be quenched by the divine intervention of Krisha, through his pearls of wisdom which stand the relentless test of time.

If even Arjuna had to submit to a force above him in times of difficulty, we are but mere humans, it is natural to seek a guiding force, tangible and intangible. The relationship between a mentor and mentee is one that is immensely special, it goes beyond the basic needs of our day to day relationships, it is one which helps us achieve self actualization, and helps us in becoming the most potent and powerful version of ourselves. If harnessed with the right person and spirit, it is bound to create wonders and leave behind a legacy.

Key notes from the chapter-

1. Mentorship is Essential for Growth – No one achieves greatness in isolation. From childhood to career, we learn through those who have walked the path before us. Mentors accelerate our journey by helping us avoid pitfalls and gain wisdom efficiently.

2. Mentorship is More Than Teaching – Unlike teachers, mentors don't just impart knowledge; they offer emotional and psychological support, inspire confidence, and nurture potential. A true mentor sees

greatness in a mentee even before they see it in themselves.

3. The Role of the Mentee is Active, Not Passive – Learning isn't just about receiving advice. The best mentees observe keenly, listen intently, and most importantly, apply what they learn. Like Eklavya from the Mahabharata, true dedication and practice can turn indirect mentorship into mastery.

4. Mentor-Mentee Relationships Evolve Over Time – A great mentor prepares the mentee to eventually surpass them. Sergey Brin and Larry Page learned from Eric Schmidt before stepping up to lead Google, while Satya Nadella took lessons from Steve Ballmer but charted his own course for Microsoft.

5. Not All Mentorships Look the Same – Some, like Steve Jobs and Tim Cook, thrive on contrasting strengths, while others, like Krishna and Arjuna, are built on deep wisdom and guidance. A mentor can be a direct teacher, a corporate leader, or even a spiritual guide.

6. Mentorship should result in the creation of an authentic and well equipped individual, not a codependent person seeking to substitute for his/her lack from the mentor- The best mentees don't replicate their mentors, they evolve the wisdom they inherit.

Chapter 3:

Focus, Flow, and Fly.

Life is a spontaneous orchestration of many activities, consumption, creation, and stagnation. The day we cease to consume, create, or stagnate, life comes to a halt and is no more. Our daily lives consist of us living within one of these modes, or even two or more simultaneously. However, when we are in the zone of creation, which is an act of movement of activity that requires our utmost attention, we sometimes drift into a sublime state of consciousness. Before I delve into explaining this state, I want to give a personal anecdote of mine, something you might relate to, in whichever contexts suit you and your passions best.

I had wanted to pursue my creative interests for the longest time; however, self-imposed limiting beliefs were causing a prolonged period of procrastination, and I even had thoughts of putting the project away for good. But on a seemingly uneventful morning, after making my daily cup of elixir, my coffee, I had this surge of inspiration flood me, it was a rush of energy and motivation, the kind of wave that hits you when you least expect it and spurs you to action.I seized the opportunity, sat down at my desk, opened my laptop, and ideas started manifesting themselves on the screen. My words flew out of my head onto the medium, and with every thought and every breath, a new sentence was given life, I was completely entranced by this wave of creativity; I ceased to think and only did, because at that moment it felt like an instinct had taken over, like an itch that was being scratched at just the right spot, it felt comfortable, primal, and it kept going, it came naturally to me, it flowed naturally.

Another instance of me getting absorbed by this state, usually happens when I'm taking a stroll across a sprawling scenery, the beauty from the nature around me taps into the rhythm in me, and it manifests itself in the form of song lyrics and song writing. With every hum of a bird, the subtle crack of leaves as a squirrel runs amok and the splendid luminescence of the water reflecting the beautiful horizon, the words flow out of me rhythmically, etching their way into my notepad in the form of verses. My best songs have always found me, not in a quiet room, but out in the world, where the earth itself seems to hum a tune only I can hear.

Yes, I'm referring to what we all collectively refer to as the state of "flow"

This is a universal experience that I am sure you have experienced at least once in life. It is a sort of state where you do and not think. It comes from our deepest instincts and consciousness and feels very comfortable and natural. It is not something you do out of obligation to others or yourself; you do it because it feels right. It's a zone that often comes frequently to some and not so frequently to others, this will be elaborated further on the later parts of the chapter, with an emphasis on how to "flow" on a regular basis.

Psychologist Mihaly Csikszentmihalyi first introduced the idea of flow in the 1970s. He described it as a state where you're fully focused, everything feels effortless, and you're performing at your best, like being "in the zone." Csikszentmihalyi discovered flow while studying happiness. He found that people feel their best when they're in this state, not just productive, but genuinely happy and fulfilled. Whether it's an athlete in a competition, an artist creating, or even someone solving a tough puzzle, flow brings out the best in us.

When you're in flow, everything just works. You're completely engrossed, and fully engaged in what you're doing, and the outside world fades away. There's no stress, no second-guessing, just pure focus and effortless action. You lose track of time, whether you're hungry, or what's happening around you. Instead, you're riding a wave of momentum, fully present in the task at hand. Your brain and body are in perfect sync, moving smoothly from one step to the next. Time either speeds up when you look at the clock and realize hours have passed without you noticing or slows down, where every moment feels rich, meaningful, and content. You're in control, energized, and performing at your best.

The idea I am trying to convey here is, that once you learn how to optimize your activities and learn to harness the art of flow, you can truly get the best out of yourself within a given time frame. Just like any other activity in the world, the flow state can not only be harnessed whenever we please, it can also be improved with practice. Like we have previously discussed in the first chapter, when we do an activity multiple times, we tend to turn it into a habit, it forms a stronger and stronger neurological connection over time, helping us to access it faster and more efficiently. Strong minds and bodies and not born that way, they are built, every day and night and every hour of the day, with every action and decision. We happen to be lucky because, it has been proven that with enough repetition and practice, you can also train your thoughts.

By learning how to tap into the state of flow, we can turn into a more productive and happy version of ourselves while also treading towards our dreams and goals. However, you might be wondering the hows and whats to how we can tap into the sublime state.

So how do you get into this powerful state of mind? Flow happens when what you're doing is just challenging enough, not so easy that you get bored and distracted, but not so difficult that you feel overwhelmed or frustrated. Imagine you're playing a video game. If the level is too easy, you'll zone out and lose interest. But if it's too hard, you'll get stuck, feel frustrated, and want to quit. The magic happens in the sweet spot, the perfect difficulty where you're pushing yourself, but still having fun. That's exactly how the flow works in real life.

Several key factors help you enter flow. First, you need a clear goal, knowing exactly what you're trying to achieve keeps your mind focused and prevents distractions. You also need instant feedback, whether it's seeing progress in your work, getting real-time reactions in a conversation, or feeling your body improve as you practice a skill. This feedback loop helps keep you engaged and motivated.

The challenge level is crucial, it needs to be balanced with your skill level. If a task is too simple, your mind will wander. If it's too complex, you'll feel anxious and stuck. But when it's right in the middle, difficult enough to be engaging but not impossible, you'll naturally fall into flow.

Another essential ingredient is minimizing distractions. If your phone is constantly buzzing, or if you're multitasking, your brain can't fully commit to the experience. Creating a focused environment helps you stay in the zone. And perhaps the most exciting part of the flow is the feeling of losing yourself in the moment. You stop overthinking, stop worrying about external things, and just *do.* Your movements, thoughts, and decisions feel effortless like they're happening naturally without force or hesitation.

Managing stress and being patient with the process is key to entering flow. If your mind is cluttered with worries, distractions, or self-doubt, it becomes much harder to fully immerse yourself in what you're doing. Flow thrives in a state of calm focus, where you're engaged but not overwhelmed. This means learning to manage stress, whether through deep breathing, mindfulness, or simply taking breaks when needed, so that you can approach tasks with a clear and open mind.

Patience is just as important. Flow isn't something you can force; it happens naturally when the right conditions are met. If you're constantly frustrated with yourself for not getting into flow quickly enough, that frustration itself becomes a barrier. Instead, trust the process. The more you practice entering flow, by finding the right challenge level, minimizing distractions, and fully engaging in your work, the easier it becomes to slip into this state of heightened productivity and enjoyment. Over time, with practice and self-awareness, you can train yourself to enter flow more easily, making it a regular and rewarding part of your life.

When all of these elements come together, flow happens. It's a deeply satisfying experience, one that leaves you feeling accomplished, fulfilled, and even happier. And the best part? Anyone can tap into it. Once you understand how the flow works and how to set yourself up for it, you'll start recognizing those moments more often, whether it's in work, hobbies, sports, or creative projects. The more you experience it, the more you'll want to chase that feeling again and again.

Sitting in a quiet corner of a coffee shop, the rich aroma of roasted beans pierced into the air, I found myself flipping through the pages of The Almanac. Somewhere between sips of my cafe latte, I landed on a section about flow state, something I'd always been curious about.

The idea was simple yet profound, real success and happiness come from doing work you truly love, the kind that pulls you in so completely that time seems to dissolve. It made perfect sense. Looking back, the moments when I've felt most productive, most alive, were the ones where I was so immersed in something that the outside world faded away.

The book emphasized that flow isn't just about efficiency, it's about fulfillment. When work feels effortless, it's often a sign that you're doing the right kind of work. On the other hand, forcing yourself through tasks you don't care about only leads to burnout. That hit home. I've seen it firsthand, the difference between dragging through a to-do list versus being so lost in something meaningful that hours slip by unnoticed.

One key takeaway stuck with me: flow isn't accidental, It can be cultivated. By cutting out distractions, designing a space for deep work, and prioritizing tasks that naturally excite you, slipping into that state becomes easier and more consistent. The idea of playing long-term games with long-term people also resonated, investing in the kind of work and relationships that sustain you over time.

I closed the book, letting the words settle. It wasn't just theory; it was a reminder. A reminder to seek work that doesn't just pay the bills but pulls me in, to embrace focus, and to chase that effortless energy where creativity thrives. The kind of work that doesn't feel like work at all.

Finally, flow and happiness are deeply connected. When you are fully present and engaged, you're not caught up in past regrets or future anxieties. Flow creates a state of deep satisfaction, making it one of the most effective ways to achieve both peak performance and lasting happiness.

Another example of someone exemplary who has mastered the art of flow in real life and has used it for professional success is James Cameron, a celebrated film director of magnum opuses such as Titanic, Terminator, and Avatar.

I picked up "Be Useful: Seven Tools for Life", written by Arnold Schwarzenegger on a quiet evening, expecting lessons on discipline and resilience. What I didn't expect was to be completely drawn into the story of James Cameron. The legendary director behind The Terminator, Jurassic Park (as a consultant), Titanic, and Avatar, is a prime example of someone who operates in a deep state of flow. His ability to fully immerse himself in his work, push creative and technological boundaries, and maintain relentless focus showcases how flow fuels innovation and success.

He is known for his intense work ethic and complete absorption in his projects. While directing The Terminator (1984), he operated under immense pressure, limited budget, tight deadlines, and industry skepticism. Yet, his deep focus allowed him to solve problems in real time, work tirelessly on set, and create a film that became a sci-fi classic. His ability to shut out distractions and immerse himself completely in his vision is a key characteristic of flow.

Flow happens when the challenge of a task matches a person's skill level. He consistently took on ambitious projects that pushed his abilities while remaining within his creative expertise. Jurassic Park (1993), though directed by Steven Spielberg, benefited from Cameron's early conceptual work in pushing the limits of CGI. His understanding of cutting-edge technology and storytelling allowed him to stay in flow, constantly innovating and refining his craft.

During Avatar (2009), He spent years developing new technology to bring his vision to life. Motion capture, 3D filming techniques, and CGI advancements were all part of the challenge. Rather than seeing these as obstacles, he became completely engrossed in solving them, demonstrating how flow enables individuals to push past limitations and create something groundbreaking. His passion for filmmaking and problem-solving kept him fully engaged, leading to a revolutionary cinematic experience.

He has also described how, when directing, he becomes so deeply involved that he loses track of time. Days on set stretch into marathon sessions where he is fully present, making decisions instinctively and without hesitation. This loss of self-consciousness and distorted sense of time are classic signs of the flow state.

His career is a testament to how flow fuels creativity, innovation, and high performance. By consistently challenging himself, eliminating distractions, and fully immersing himself in his work, he has been able to create some of the most influential films in cinematic history. His journey demonstrates that when passion and skill align with the right level of challenge, the result is nothing short of extraordinary.

While talking about the creative state of flow, It would be blasphemous to exclude mention of the celebrated artist, Vincent Van Gogh.

He lived in a near-constant state of flow, pouring his emotions and energy into his art with intense focus. He often painted for hours without stopping, completely absorbed in his work, sometimes finishing entire pieces in a single day. His bold colors and expressive brushstrokes were not just artistic choices but reflections of his deep emotional connection to his craft. He constantly challenged himself, experimenting with light, movement, and technique, keeping his creativity sharp and engaged. He would lose all sense of time, even painting through the night with candles strapped to his hat. Despite his personal struggles, his ability to enter flow allowed him to create over 2,100 works, leaving behind a legacy of passion-driven brilliance. His story is a testament to how flow fuels creativity, purpose, and extraordinary achievement.

The ability to focus so deeply into the act of creating, results in a state of flow, which in turn helps us fly.

Flow isn't just a tool for productivity or success, it's a way of being, a doorway to our most authentic and powerful selves. It's in those moments when we're so deeply immersed in something we love that we forget everything else, our doubts, our limitations, even the ticking clock. Whether it's James Cameron pushing the boundaries of cinema, Van Gogh pouring his soul onto the canvas, or simply you, lost in your craft, flow is where the magic happens.

I feel familiarized with the state of flow now, after years of consistently working towards intentionally drifting into the state. I've realized it's the art of losing yourself to find yourself. that rush of inspiration, the effortless rhythm where thoughts and actions align perfectly. And I bet you have too. Maybe in writing, painting, coding, running, or even having a deep conversation. Those are the moments when we aren't just doing, we are being. Time disappears, resistance fades, and we become pure creation.

Flow isn't something reserved for the geniuses of the world, it's within all of us. The more we learn to tap into it, the more we break free from distraction, fear, and hesitation. The more we let go, the more we become. So chase that feeling. Cultivate it. Because in flow, we don't just create our best work, we create our best selves.

Key notes from the chapter-

1. Flow is a Natural State of Effortless Creation.
2. When you're in flow, you don't force creativity, it happens naturally. Your mind and body synchronize, and you act without hesitation, free from distractions and self-doubt.
3. The Right Balance of Challenge and Skill Unlocks Flow.
4. Flow happens when an activity is challenging enough to engage you but not so difficult that it causes frustration. Finding that "sweet spot" keeps you fully immersed and performing at your best.
5. Repetition and Habit Strengthen Your Ability to Access Flow.
6. Just like any skill, the ability to enter flow can be trained. Through consistent practice, the neurological connections that enable flow become stronger, making it easier to reach this state.
7. Eliminating Distractions and Managing Stress Helps You Stay in Flow.
8. A cluttered mind is the enemy of flow. Reducing external distractions, managing stress, and staying present in the moment create the perfect conditions for deep focus and creative immersion.
9. Flow is the Key to Fulfillment and Peak Performance.
10. Whether you're an artist, an athlete, or a filmmaker like James Cameron, flow fuels creativity and

innovation. It brings happiness, purpose, and mastery over your craft.

11. Flow is for Everyone, Not Just Geniuses.

12. The magic of flow isn't limited to extraordinary people; it's within everyone. The more you cultivate it, the more you unlock your true potential, both in your work and in your life.

Chapter 4:
The Power of Daily Habits

I believe a lot of facets that are being covered intensively in this book, only have value worth a penny if they are not being materialized in your everyday life. An essential feature of the book, the core of this material lies in the power of habits and how they transform one's mind, body and environment. Habits are simple conceptually, however, when it comes to implementing them in everyday life, we seem to hit a stump. We have tall tales of excuses that come up when we try to justify why we weren't able to stick to a certain routine or build a habit, every bundle of excuses is just a facade, masking deeper psychological obstacles, such as fear of change, perfectionism, self-doubt, or limiting beliefs rooted in our past experiences. Overcoming these barriers isn't just about pushing harder; it's about recognizing and addressing the underlying issues that keep us stuck in old patterns. This will be delved into in the later chapters, specifically, chapters 5 and 6. where we will examine the psychological mechanisms behind resistance to change and how to systematically dismantle these barriers.

Several habits are taught to us from our childhood, which claim to help us lead a healthy and prosperous life. Some of them include waking up early in the morning, maintaining a tidy space, eating healthy food, and working out. Some of us follow them blindly, whereas the rest question the legitimacy behind these standardized practices. You might think, how does cleaning up my space, maintaining a healthy diet and working out every day help me in establishing a successful finance startup? As much as we would like to deny it, every aspect of our life seeps into the other, it is the interconnectedness of our life, we are whole, not an individual sum of smaller facets. The brain still happens to be one of the biggest enigmas to date, this complex organ functions in the strangest ways, some answered by science and others by strange mystical beliefs. When you push yourself into doing difficult things every day, habitually, you get hardwired to do difficult things in general. Let me give you an example of a woman named Daisy.

Daisy wanted to start her own design firm. She had her ideas and plans laid out, but she lacked the faith and belief that she could establish a successful business. Her low self-esteem and insecurities deteriorated her mental health. One day, she happened to read a fitness column in a magazine that claimed running every day could drastically improve one's mental well-being. She wanted to give it a try since there was no harm in running. "I might even get in shape before next summer!" she thought to herself. Every day, she put on her gym tights, sports t-shirt, a pair of running shoes, and wore a pedometer to keep track of her progress. In the initial days, she barely covered one to two kilometers at a time. It was tiring; her muscles ached, and her heart felt like it was about to give out at any moment. But it felt nice to be outside, and it was a low-cost, fun activity, so she stuck with it. Some days, she was able to cover up to 3 kilometers; other days, it was barely 2. However, after a couple of weeks, she got used to running and set a goal of being able to run 5 kilometers at least twice a week. Once she achieved her small goal, she eventually decided to try 10 kilometers. Soon after her first 10K, she was onto her next goal of a half marathon. Running was not inherently rewarding; she won no prizes or received accolades, but she realized something, it was teaching her discipline, patience, and persistence. It takes a good amount of physical strength and endurance to run long distances, but more than anything, it takes an enormous amount of mental endurance. She developed great pride and confidence, knowing that she could run a good distance. This not only improved her physical and mental health but also gave her newfound confidence. She used the courage she developed through her healthy habit and finally started actualizing her dream of starting a design firm, which she had wanted to pursue for ages.

Discipline and routine are very underrated traits to develop, they are sometimes confused with the authoritarian way of leading life or leading a bland and monotonous life, which is quite the contrary. Discipline gives us the power to break out of habits and practices which no longer serve us, through discipline, we can adhere to the plan we lay out for reaching our goals. Routine helps us live in the present, it helps us function effectively even in our lowest of days, it helps us remember our goals on our happiest of days, it brings about a state of equilibrium in our lives, a structure and a sort of layout which guides us to our dreams.

With Daisy's example, we see how discipline and routine in running helped her towards her long-term goal of starting her firm. This brings us to how physical fitness and other good habits can snowball into other facets of life, making other experiences better.

Mental challenges can be overcome through good physical health. A structured fitness regimen builds resilience, instills self-discipline, and enhances mental well-being, helping individuals push through limitations. Paralympic athletes exemplify this principle, as their unwavering commitment to training enables them to surpass physical disabilities with mental strength. For example, Nick Mayhugh, diagnosed with cerebral palsy, became a world-record-holding Paralympic sprinter, demonstrating that a strong mindset can turn adversity into achievement. Similarly, Tatyana McFadden, born with spina bifida, has won multiple Paralympic medals in wheelchair racing, showcasing the power of discipline and self-belief. These athletes exemplify how physical fitness strengthens mental endurance, allowing individuals to push beyond their perceived limitations and achieve greatness.

It is fascinating to note that those who are physically challenged, often develop a bulletproof mindset to counteract their physical limitations, it is essential for an abled individual to draw inspiration from those who have it harder in life, but still push through to leave a longstanding mark on their pursuits. True strength lies in balancing both mind and body, compensating for what we lack to achieve our fullest potential.

A healthy mind often results in a healthy body and vice versa, the key to both is a nourished mind and body. Our nutrition has a huge role to play in our mental and physical health. Inarguably, the key to longevity and peak physical performance is nutrition and sleep. The food we eat is of tremendous significance. In the name of convenience, we put highly processed and nutritionally deficient food into our body. We often prioritize the urgency of the present, rather than considering the longevity and health of our future. We are what we eat is an age-old sermon, yet, in today's fast-paced world we barely have time to nourish our body adequately.

I was undeniably in the same place as everybody else; all it took was a long bout of flu that brought me to my senses. A seemingly simple disease like the flu is very easy to manage, given that your body has adequate nutrition, hydration, and rest. However, due to my previously poor eating habits and sleep cycle, I was bedridden for almost a week. It was quite a humbling experience. When you're in poor health, all urgency flies right out the window; we are left with our ailing bodies and our thoughts. While I was bedridden, all I could think about was how I could have avoided this condition if I had just allowed my body to rest and effectively nourished myself. The content you will read further is a strong emphasis on the need for adequate nutrition amongst us, the food we eat, inevitably decides how our body copes with environmental and psychological stresses. For a start, start by prioritizing nutritionally dense meals, reduce processed food and aim for a macro and micro-nutrient balanced food.

Now, to address the question of How Nutrition Supports Habit Formation and Discipline, I have to take you down the burrow of science for a thorough understanding, there happens to be a reason why I frequently bring up factual and verified scientific pieces of information. It is because, when scientific information is combined with supportive strategies, it can enhance the likelihood of adopting new habits. Plus, it just happens to itch the side of my head that likes to constantly question everything and quenches my why, when, and hows.

What we eat has a direct impact on our ability to build and maintain habits. Good nutrition fuels the brain, stabilizes emotions, and strengthens willpower, all of which play a key role in staying disciplined. By making smart dietary choices, we can create the right conditions for long-term success in habit formation.

Blood Sugar Stability and Willpower-

Ever noticed how a sugar rush feels great at first but is quickly followed by a crash? Foods high in refined sugar and processed carbs cause rapid blood sugar spikes, leading to fatigue, brain fog, and impulsivity. This makes it harder to make thoughtful decisions and stick to good habits.

In contrast, protein, healthy fats, and fiber-rich foods keep blood sugar levels stable, providing steady energy throughout the day. This stability supports better impulse control and decision-making, making it easier to follow through on daily routines. Roy Baumeister's 2011 research on willpower, often referred to as ego depletion theory, suggests that willpower is a finite resource that gets drained throughout the day as we make decisions and exert self-control. His studies indicate that when people repeatedly use willpower, whether resisting temptation, making difficult choices, or focusing on tasks, they experience mental fatigue, making it harder to maintain discipline. However, by choosing nutrient-dense foods, we can sustain self-discipline and strengthen our ability to stick to habits.

His findings highlight the strong connection between blood sugar stability and decision-making, reinforcing the idea that maintaining good nutrition isn't just about physical health, it's essential for mental resilience and habit formation as well.

Gut-Brain Connection and Mood Regulation-

The gut isn't just responsible for digestion, it also plays a huge role in mental health and motivation. The gut microbiome helps produce neurotransmitters like serotonin and dopamine, which influence mood, focus, and consistency. A well-balanced gut improves emotional regulation, reducing stress and making it easier to stay on track with positive habits.

Eating fermented foods (like yogurt, pickles, and kimchi), fiber, and prebiotics supports a healthy gut, which in turn helps maintain motivation and self-discipline. When your gut is happy, your brain functions better, and sticking to habits feels more natural.

Protein and Neurotransmitter Support-

Protein is often associated solely with muscle-building, but it's also crucial for mental clarity and habit formation. Amino acids from protein are the building blocks of dopamine, the neurotransmitter responsible for motivation, focus, and reward-seeking behavior. Without enough protein, dopamine production can drop, leading to low motivation and difficulty forming new habits.

Starting the day with a high-protein breakfast can boost focus, reduce cravings, and set a disciplined tone for the rest of the day. Whether it's eggs, Greek yogurt, or a protein smoothie, this simple habit can have a major impact on productivity and willpower. Plus, protein keeps you feeling fuller for the rest of the day, which can drastically reduce your unhealthy binges throughout the day.

Omega-3 Fatty Acids and Cognitive Function-

Omega-3 fatty acids, found in fish, walnuts, and flaxseeds, are essential for brain health, focus, and habit formation. These healthy fats reduce brain inflammation and enhance neuroplasticity, which is the brain's ability to adapt and form new neural pathways. This makes it easier to develop and strengthen good habits over time.

By optimizing nutrition, we can fuel our brain, regulate our emotions, and strengthen our discipline, making it far easier to build the habits that lead to long-term success.

Another key factor in optimizing our mental and physical health is sleep. It might seem trivial in comparison to everything else we have covered so far, but it just so happens to be a really important factor in our overall health and well-being. When we sleep, our body undergoes vital processes for restoration and health. Physically, muscles repair, bones strengthen, and the immune system boosts, while energy stores replenish. The brain consolidates memories, processes emotions, and clears toxins, enhancing cognitive function and mental well-being. Sleep also regulates hormones, balancing stress, appetite, and growth. These processes improve learning, mood, and overall health while reducing the risk of chronic diseases. Without quality sleep, both body and mind suffer, leading to impaired function and long-term health issues.

A good night's slumber is a fundamental pillar of success, playing a crucial role in habit formation, self-discipline, and goal achievement. When we sleep, our brain strengthens neural connections, making it easier to develop and sustain positive habits. Studies show that lack of sleep disrupts the basal ganglia, a key brain region for habit formation, making it harder to stick to routines.

Sleep also directly impacts productivity and goal achievement by enhancing focus, creativity, and problem-solving skills. Well-rested individuals perform better in work, sports, and personal development because they have the mental clarity and emotional stability to stay motivated and push through challenges.

Instead of viewing sleep as wasted time, it should be seen as an investment in cognitive and physical well-being. By maintaining a consistent sleep schedule and reducing nighttime distractions, individuals can accelerate their progress toward achieving their goals.

Moving on to perhaps, the core of the chapter's essence, the scientific basis of habit formation. Forming good habits isn't just about willpower, it's about how our brains work. Science shows that habits develop through a process called the habit loop, a concept introduced by Charles Duhigg in The Power of Habit which includes three steps: cue, routine, and reward. The cue is what triggers the habit (like seeing your running shoes by the door), the routine is the action itself (going for a run), and the reward is what reinforces it (feeling energized afterward). Over time, repeating this loop makes the habit automatic.

Our brains actually rewire themselves when we repeat behaviors. This happens through synaptic plasticity, meaning the more we do something, the stronger the neural connections become (Hebb's Rule). Eventually, these actions move from the decision-making part of the brain or the prefrontal cortex to the basal ganglia, which handles automatic behaviors. This is why habits, good or bad, feel natural once they are ingrained.

Another key factor in building habits is environment design. Studies show that our surroundings heavily influence behavior. Want to drink more water? Keep a bottle on your desk. Want to eat healthier? Put fruit at eye level in the fridge. James Clear, in Atomic Habits, calls this "habit stacking" and "environment shaping" to make good habits easier. Research from Stanford's Behavior Design Lab supports this, showing that small, intentional changes in our environment significantly boost habit formation.

The time it takes to form a habit varies depending on the complexity of the behavior and individual differences. A 2009 study by Phillippa Lally and colleagues at University College London, published in the European Journal of Social Psychology, found that on average, it takes 66 days for a new habit to become automatic. However, this number isn't fixed, simpler habits, like drinking a glass of water after waking up, can become ingrained in as little as 18 days, while more complex habits, such as daily exercise, can take up to 254 days to fully solidify. The key takeaway is that consistency, rather than perfection, is what ultimately makes a habit stick.

Further reinforcing the power of habits, Wendy Wood, a researcher at the University of Southern California, found that about 43% of our daily actions are habitual rather than consciously chosen . This means nearly half of what we do each day is driven by repeated behaviors that we've performed so often they no longer require active thought. These findings highlight how habits shape our routines and why intentional habit formation is crucial for long-term success.

The process of habit formation relies on context and repetition. The more frequently a behavior is repeated in a stable environment, the stronger the associated neural pathways become, making it easier to sustain over time. This is why environmental cues play a crucial role, placing your running shoes by the door can serve as a trigger to exercise, just as brushing your teeth before bed signals sleep preparation.

Ultimately, habit formation isn't about an exact timeline but about persistence and consistency. If you miss a day, it doesn't erase progress. What matters is getting back on track and continuing to reinforce the habit until it becomes second nature.

The takeaway? Good habits don't form overnight, but by using cues, repetition, and setting up the right environment, you can make them stick. Instead of relying on motivation, which fades, build habits that become second nature.

A book that comes to my mind whenever I think of how habits lead to success, is inevitably "bounce" a book penned by Matthew syed.

In Bounce, Matthew dismantles the myth that success is purely the result of innate talent. Instead, he argues that habit, routine, and deliberate practice are the real foundations of greatness. He highlights how world-class athletes, musicians, and artists achieve mastery not through natural ability alone but through structured, repetitive training and a disciplined mindset. Syed emphasizes the 10,000-hour rule, clarifying that success isn't just about repetition, it's about purposeful, high-quality practice with constant feedback and refinement.

Routine plays a critical role in skill development. Successful individuals cultivate automatic, repeatable behaviors that help them perform under pressure without hesitation. Athletes like David Beckham and Roger Federer didn't rely on raw talent; they designed strict routines that allowed them to fine-tune their abilities over time. A well-structured routine removes decision fatigue, making practice and improvement second nature rather than dependent on motivation.

Another key concept in the book is the growth mindset, which suggests that abilities are developed through effort rather than being fixed traits. Those who believe in continuous learning and adaptation tend to persist longer in their practice, while those who think talent is static often give up when faced with obstacles. Syed also highlights the importance of failure in the habit-building process. The best performers analyze their mistakes, adjust their training methods, and use setbacks as stepping stones rather than as deterrents.

Ultimately, Bounce proves that success is built on consistent, disciplined habits rather than sheer talent. By following structured routines, focusing on deliberate skill-building, and using failure as feedback, anyone can achieve remarkable improvement. Success isn't about being born great, it's about building the right habits over time and committing to continuous growth and refinement.

Daisy's story isn't just about running, it's about rewriting the narrative we tell ourselves. She didn't start out believing she could run a marathon, just like she didn't start out believing she could build a business. But step by step, day by day, she proved to herself that she could do hard things. That's the power of habits. They're not just routines; they're daily affirmations of who we are becoming.

Whether it's the grit of Paralympic athletes defying expectations, the fuel we give our bodies through nutrition, or the simple discipline of a good night's sleep, every small choice we make is shaping our future. Science backs it up, lasting change doesn't come from bursts of motivation but from the quiet, consistent work we put in every day. It's about setting ourselves up for success, designing environments that nudge us in the right direction, and trusting that even the smallest steps forward will lead to something bigger.

The truth is, we don't just wake up one day as the person we dream of becoming—we build that person, habit by habit, choice by choice. And when we commit to that process, we don't just change what we do. We change who we are.

Key notes from the chapter-

1. Habits Shape Our Lives – Success isn't about isolated efforts but about daily habits that transform our mind, body, and environment. Small, consistent actions compound over time.

2. Discipline and Routine Build Mental Strength – Engaging in difficult tasks regularly, like exercise, reinforces resilience, confidence, and perseverance, which transfer to other areas of life.

3. Physical and Mental Health Are Interconnected – Good nutrition, sleep, and fitness enhance mental endurance, willpower, and emotional stability, making it easier to stay disciplined.

4. Science Supports Habit Formation – Habits follow a loop (cue, routine, reward), and repetition strengthens neural pathways, making behaviors automatic over time. Environment design helps reinforce positive habits.

5. Growth Mindset and Persistence Matter – Success isn't based on talent but on consistent, high-quality effort. Learning from failure and maintaining a structured routine lead to long-term improvement.

6. We Become Our Daily Choices – The habits we build define our identity. Lasting change isn't about motivation but about showing up consistently and committing to progress every day.

Chapter 5:

Overcoming Anxieties and Depression: Tough Days Make Us Tougher.

Life is an unpredictable journey filled with both highs and lows. While happiness and success bring us joy, challenges and hardships test our resilience. The reality is that struggles are temporary, but our capacity to overcome them is what defines us.

If you've ever felt lost, overwhelmed, or as if the weight of the world is pressing down on you, know that you are not alone. Every single person goes through moments of self-doubt, fear, and emotional pain. Some days, the burden seems unbearable, and it feels as though the darkness will never lift. But here's the truth, no storm lasts forever. Pain is not a permanent state of being.

Unfortunately, many individuals today are finding it increasingly difficult to navigate emotional distress, leading to an alarming rise in anxiety, depression, and even tragic cases of suicide. We hear heartbreaking stories of young, brilliant minds at top universities like IITs, IIMs, and Ivy League institutions succumbing to the pressures of academic and societal expectations. We see professionals burning out, feeling trapped in a relentless cycle of stress. And beyond the statistics, there are real people, friends, family members, colleagues. who silently suffer, unsure of how to escape the mental battles they face daily.

Why do we allow emotions to consume us so deeply? Why do we feel trapped by our own thoughts? The answer lies in how the human brain has evolved. It was designed to detect threats, to prepare us for survival. But in today's world, where threats are more psychological than physical, our brains sometimes misinterpret stress, amplifying it to extreme levels. This leads to chronic worry, emotional paralysis, and, in some cases, despair.

The good news is that there is a way out. There are proven methods to regain control over our minds, to quiet the chaos within, and to build resilience so that even in the darkest moments, we can find a way forward.

One of the biggest reasons why so many people struggle with mental health today is unrealistic societal expectations. From a young age, we are told that success is defined by our academic performance, the job we secure, and how much money we make. But what about happiness? What about mental peace? The pressure to meet these rigid standards often leaves us feeling inadequate, even when we achieve great things. We become so focused on external validation that we neglect our own emotional needs.

Then there's digital overload and social comparison. We live in an era where social media has become an inescapable part of life. While it connects us, it also constantly exposes us to curated versions of other people's lives, highlight reels that make our own struggles feel more isolating. We see influencers traveling the world, peers celebrating achievements, and friends appearing happier than ever. This fuels anxiety, making us feel like we're always falling short. Comparison tends to lower our self esteem, further creating self limiting beliefs in our subconscious minds, comparison is the thief of joy, and rightly called so, because it makes it less about what we can do with what we have and more about what others have.

What we fail to realize is that these platforms rarely showcase the full picture. The person posting a perfect selfie might be battling their own silent demons.

Despite living in a hyperconnected digital world, many of us feel more isolated than ever. The paradox of technology is that while it bridges physical distances, it often deepens emotional disconnection. Instead of having meaningful face-to-face conversations, we resort to texting and scrolling through feeds. True human connection; where we feel seen, heard, and valued, is becoming rare, leaving many people struggling with loneliness despite being surrounded by virtual connections.

Academic pressure also play a significant role in deteriorating mental health. Whether it's the race for higher grades or the relentless pursuit of promotions, the pressure to perform is relentless. Students feel the weight of their parents' expectations, professionals fear losing their jobs, and entrepreneurs constantly battle self-doubt. The need to be "successful" in the traditional sense has made failure seem unacceptable. But failure is a part of growth, it is not a reflection of one's worth.

In today's competitive corporate landscape, the rise of perfectionism and reduced tolerance for failure have negatively impacted mental health and resilience. Employees often feel pressured to perform flawlessly, leading to anxiety, burnout, and a fear of taking risks, stifling creativity and adaptability. In contrast, companies like Google promote a culture of psychological safety, where failure is seen as a learning opportunity. Through initiatives like "20% time" for passion projects, mental health support, and open dialogue around setbacks, Google fosters innovation while supporting employee well-being. This approach highlights the importance of workplace culture in building resilience and sustaining mental health.

Another major problem is the lack of emotional resilience training. We spend years in school learning complex mathematical formulas and scientific principles, but where do we learn how to manage stress, overcome self-doubt, or cope with failure? Emotional resilience isn't something we are born with, it's a skill that must be developed. Yet, most educational systems do not prioritize teaching these essential life skills, leaving individuals unprepared to handle the inevitable challenges of life. We spend hours planning for a week-long trip, carefully packing for every possibility, yet we rarely invest the same effort in preparing for life's challenges. Emotional resilience, like character, is a skill that can be developed with intention and practice. It helps us navigate stress, failure, and change, yet we often leave it to chance. If we prepared for inner strength the way we prepare for travel, we'd be far better equipped to handle life's journey.

Lastly, there's the neglect of mental well-being in traditional education. Schools and universities put tremendous emphasis on intelligence, but what about emotional intelligence? The ability to manage emotions, deal with conflicts, and handle stress is just as crucial, if not more, than academic excellence. Teaching young minds how to process their feelings and navigate life's hurdles can significantly reduce mental health struggles in adulthood. Imagine a world where children grow up knowing that their self-worth isn't tied to grades or external achievements, but to their ability to handle challenges with resilience and self-awareness.

The Need for Emotional Intelligence in Education

While schools emphasize academic excellence, they often neglect one of the most crucial life skills, emotional intelligence. Children may excel in math and science, but without the ability to manage stress, navigate conflicts, or cope with anxiety, they may struggle in adulthood. Emotional resilience isn't just a soft skill; it's a critical foundation for mental well-being, decision-making, and healthy relationships. Integrating emotional intelligence training into education could equip students with the tools to handle life's challenges with confidence and self-awareness.

One way schools can foster emotional resilience is through mindfulness programs, which teach children how to stay present and manage stress effectively. Simple practices like breathing exercises or guided meditation can help students regulate emotions and reduce anxiety. Additionally, conflict resolution training can empower them with the skills to navigate disagreements in a healthy and constructive manner, preventing small disputes from escalating into major issues.

Children should be taught the art of negotiation early, not just to "get their way," but to understand how to communicate needs, compromise, and create mutually beneficial outcomes. Negotiation teaches them that even if they can't get everything they want, they can still find value in a situation. This skill builds emotional resilience by helping children manage disappointment, reduce conflict, and stay solution-focused. It encourages empathy (seeing the other side), assertiveness (expressing their needs), and flexibility (adjusting expectations), all crucial for thriving in both personal and social settings. By normalizing negotiation in schools through group projects, peer interactions, or conflict resolution, kids learn that setbacks aren't the end, just opportunities to rethink, reframe, and re-engage.

Beyond conflict management, students also need practical coping mechanisms for stress. Workshops on managing pressure, whether from academics, social expectations, or personal struggles, can provide them with real-world tools to stay balanced. Implementing emotional intelligence curriculums that focus on self-awareness, empathy, negotiation and communication skills can further enhance their ability to connect with others and understand their own emotions.

Finally, mental health awareness programs can help remove the stigma around emotional struggles, encouraging open conversations about well-being. When students learn that it's okay to talk about their feelings and seek support, they develop healthier relationships with their emotions. By integrating these programs into education, we can raise a generation that is not only intellectually capable but also emotionally strong, better equipped to navigate life's hardships with resilience and confidence, also adept at negotiation when the circumstances call for it.

How to Regain Control Over Our Minds

Tackling anxiety and depression requires a structured, multi-dimensional approach that integrates psychology, neuroscience, and personal discipline. One of the most effective ways to regain control over our emotions is through mindfulness and meditation. Mindfulness encourages us to be fully present in the moment without judgment, allowing us to observe our thoughts and emotions without becoming overwhelmed by them. Scientific research has shown that meditation not only reduces stress but also enhances focus and rewires the brain for positivity by increasing gray matter density in areas associated with emotional regulation, such as the prefrontal cortex. Simple practices like starting with 5–10 minutes of guided meditation daily, focusing on the breath when feeling anxious, or engaging in mindful activities such as walking,exercising, eating healthy, or deep listening can help cultivate a sense of calm. Mindfulness teaches us to detach from overthinking and redirect our attention to productive actions rather than ruminating on negative thoughts.

Another powerful tool for managing anxiety and depression is Cognitive Behavioral Therapy (CBT). As one of the most effective therapeutic approaches, CBT helps individuals recognize and reframe negative thought patterns, replacing them with healthier perspectives. Techniques such as journaling can be particularly helpful in identifying recurring negative thoughts and challenging them with more balanced viewpoints. The "5-4-3-2-1" grounding technique, which engages all five senses, is useful in breaking out of anxious spirals.The 5-4-3-2-1 grounding technique is a simple yet powerful tool to reduce anxiety and build emotional resilience by reconnecting with the present moment through the five senses. It involves naming 5 things you can see, 4 you can feel, 3 you can hear, 2 you can smell, and 1 you can taste. This sensory check-in helps calm racing thoughts, center the mind, and bring a sense of control during stress. It's especially useful for children and adults alike, offering a quick and effective way to self-regulate and stay grounded.

Exposure therapy, where fears are faced gradually instead of avoided, helps rewire the brain's response to anxiety triggers. Additionally, practicing thought challenging, where irrational fears are replaced with logical reasoning, enables individuals to cultivate a more rational and constructive mindset. By consistently applying these techniques, individuals can gradually shift from automatic negative thinking to a more empowering and resilient outlook.For a deeper understanding of Cognitive Behavioral Therapy (CBT), it is recommended that you consult with a licensed mental health professional.

Gratitude and positive psychology play a crucial role in fostering emotional well-being. Studies have shown that practicing gratitude increases the production of dopamine and serotonin, neurotransmitters responsible for happiness, helping to rewire the brain for positivity. By shifting focus from what's lacking to what's abundant, the mind begins to perceive challenges as opportunities for growth rather than insurmountable obstacles. Simple habits such as maintaining a gratitude journal, expressing appreciation to someone daily, or reflecting on three positive moments from each day before sleeping can reinforce this mindset. Even something as small as shifting self-talk from "I have to" to "I get to" can transform obligations into privileges, promoting a more grateful and fulfilled perspective on life.

Finally, physical well-being is deeply intertwined with mental health, and neglecting it often exacerbates emotional distress. Prioritizing sleep hygiene by ensuring 7–9 hours of quality rest each night helps regulate mood and cognitive function. Nutrition also plays a key role, with diets rich in omega-3 fatty acids and antioxidants being linked to improved mental health. Regular exercise, even just 30 minutes of physical activity daily, has been shown to release endorphins, which act as natural mood enhancers. Additionally, exposure to sunlight is essential, as vitamin D deficiency has been strongly linked to depression. Incorporating these physical health practices into daily life can provide a strong foundation for emotional resilience, making it easier to manage anxiety and depression effectively. By integrating mindfulness, CBT techniques, gratitude, and physical well-being into daily routines, individuals can cultivate a balanced, empowered, and mentally resilient life.

The Silva Method: Reprogramming the Subconscious Mind

Many of us struggle with self-doubt, limiting beliefs, and mental barriers that hold us back from reaching our true potential. Whether it's anxiety, fear of failure, or a negative self-image, these internal obstacles often feel insurmountable. However, what if the key to breaking free lies within our own minds? The Silva Method, developed by José Silva, is a powerful yet lesser-known technique designed to reprogram the subconscious, helping us develop focus, creativity, and self-healing through deep relaxation and visualization. By learning to access and influence our subconscious mind, we can overcome inner resistance and take control of our thoughts, emotions, and actions.

One of the foundational techniques of the Silva Method is Alpha State Training. Most of us operate in a high-alert, beta brainwave state throughout the day, which can lead to stress and overthinking. The Silva Method teaches us how to shift into the alpha state, a relaxed yet focused mode where our brain functions more efficiently for problem-solving and creativity. This state is often associated with deep meditation, where the mind becomes more receptive to positive change. By practicing techniques to enter the alpha state, such as deep breathing and guided relaxation, we can break free from patterns of anxiety, allowing us to think clearly and respond to challenges with confidence.

Another key element of the Silva Method is Creative Visualization. Have you ever noticed how powerful our thoughts are? When we constantly dwell on failure or negative outcomes, we reinforce those patterns in our subconscious, making them more likely to occur. Creative visualization reverses this process by using the imagination to create positive mental images of success. Whether it's visualizing yourself confidently delivering a speech, achieving a fitness goal, or overcoming social anxiety, the brain begins to perceive these images as reality, strengthening the neural pathways associated with success. Athletes, performers, and top professionals use this technique to enhance their abilities, and we can apply it to any area of our lives where we feel blocked or limited. In *High Performance* by Jake Humphrey and Professor Daniel Hughes, they discuss the powerful impact of visualization in achieving success. For example, they suggest that football players, when feeling low or lacking confidence, can visualize themselves achieving their goal, scoring a crucial goal, making a successful pass, or winning the game. By vividly imagining these scenarios, players can activate the same neural pathways as if they were actually performing the actions, boosting their belief and emotional resilience. This mental rehearsal helps enhance focus, reduce anxiety, and reframe negative thoughts, ultimately improving performance when faced with real challenges.

Affirmations and self-suggestions are another essential part of the Silva Method. The subconscious mind is constantly absorbing the messages we send it, both positive and negative. If we tell ourselves, *"I'll never be good enough"* or *"I always fail,"* we reinforce those beliefs. However, by consciously replacing these thoughts with empowering affirmations like *"I am capable and resilient"* or *"I trust myself to handle challenges,"* we can reprogram our subconscious to work for us rather than against us. Repeating these affirmations daily, especially in a relaxed alpha state, allows them to sink deeply into the subconscious, gradually shifting our mindset toward self-belief and success.

Lastly, Mental Rehearsal is an incredibly effective tool for boosting confidence and motivation. Just as athletes practice their moves in their minds before stepping onto the field, we can mentally rehearse positive outcomes for any challenge we face. If you struggle with public speaking, for instance, you can visualize yourself standing in front of an audience, speaking clearly and confidently, receiving warm applause. By experiencing this success in your mind first, you reduce fear and self-doubt when the actual moment arrives. Your subconscious starts to believe that you've already succeeded, making real-world performance feel much more natural and effortless.

The beauty of the Silva Method is that it puts the power back in our hands. Instead of feeling trapped by our mental barriers, we can actively reprogram our subconscious to align with our goals, dreams, and highest potential. The mind is an incredibly powerful tool, when we learn to use it to our advantage, there are no limits to what we can achieve.

Vishen Lakhiani's Journey: A Case Study in Mental Mastery and Personal Growth

We all have moments when we feel stuck, trapped by limiting beliefs, self-doubt, and the fear that we're not capable of more. Vishen Lakhiani, the founder of Mindvalley, was once in that place. Coming from humble beginnings, he faced financial struggles and career setbacks that made success seem like a distant dream. But instead of accepting those limitations, he decided to reprogram his mind, changing his internal dialogue, practicing visualization, and using meditation to reshape his reality. Today, he leads one of the world's most influential personal growth companies, proving that success isn't about luck or background, it's about mastering the mind.

One of the most powerful lessons from Vishen's journey is that the mind is programmable. Too often, we live by subconscious narratives that tell us we're not good enough, smart enough, or deserving of success. Vishen realized these were just stories, ones that could be rewritten. By actively challenging and replacing limiting beliefs, he shifted his mindset from scarcity to possibility. The same applies to us: when we become aware of our negative thought patterns and intentionally replace them with empowering beliefs, we change how we see ourselves and what we believe we can achieve.

A key tool in Vishen's transformation was meditation and visualization. Instead of just working harder, he trained his mind to see success before it happened. By vividly imagining his future self, successful, confident, and thriving. He primed his brain to recognize and seize opportunities that aligned with that vision. Neuroscience backs this up: our brains don't distinguish between real and imagined experiences, so the more we visualize success, the more our subconscious starts working to make it real. This means that if we want to break free from mental barriers, we must first create a clear mental picture of where we want to go and immerse ourselves in that vision daily.

One of the biggest shifts Vishen made was understanding that success follows emotional mastery, not the other way around. Many of us believe that once we achieve our goals, whether it's financial stability, career growth, or personal fulfillment, then we'll feel confident and happy. But Vishen discovered the opposite to be true: when we cultivate emotional resilience, gratitude, and inner peace first, external success naturally follows. Instead of chasing achievements in the hope of feeling fulfilled, he focused on mastering his emotions and appreciating life in the present. This shift in perspective is powerful because it means that no matter where we are in life, we have control over our emotional well-being, and that foundation makes success inevitable.

Of course, Vishen's journey wasn't without struggles. Like anyone else, he faced failures and moments of doubt. But what set him apart was resilience and consistency. He understood that setbacks weren't signs to quit; they were lessons pushing him towards growth. Rather than letting obstacles define him, he used them as fuel to keep evolving. This is a crucial takeaway for anyone facing challenges, resilience isn't about avoiding failure, but about learning, adapting, and moving forward with even more clarity and strength.

At its core, Vishen's story is a testament to the fact that we are not victims of our circumstances, we are creators of our reality. If we learn to reprogram our thoughts, visualize our success, master our emotions, and stay resilient through challenges, we can break through any mental barrier standing in our way. The same tools that transformed Vishen's life are available to all of us. The question is: are we ready to use them?

Resilience is a Skill, Not a Trait. Just like everything we have previously discussed earlier, habits are revolutionary, be it physical, mental, or behavioral. Through consistent and intentional actions and routine, we are bound to revolutionize our lives.

We all face moments when life feels overwhelming, when anxiety, doubt, and setbacks make us question our own strength. But the truth is, difficult days do not define us; how we rise above them does. Struggles with mental health can feel all-consuming, but they are not permanent. What is permanent, however, is our ability to grow through them, to develop resilience, and to emerge stronger than before.

Resilience isn't something we're born with, it's something we build. Just like learning a new language or training a muscle, we can strengthen our ability to handle stress, reframe negative thoughts, and regain control over our emotions. By integrating mindfulness, emotional intelligence, and self-programming techniques into our daily lives, we can shift from merely coping with life's challenges to actively shaping our mindset and future. Mental well-being is not a battle to be fought; it's a skill to be mastered.

To start, we must learn to view setbacks as lessons rather than failures. Every challenge carries an opportunity to grow, even when it doesn't feel that way in the moment. Mindfulness and emotional intelligence should become daily habits, helping us stay present, self-aware, and in control of our reactions. Just as we prioritize physical health, eating well, exercising, and getting enough sleep, mental health should be treated with the same level of care and attention.

Another crucial shift is reprogramming negative self-talk. Instead of letting doubt control us, we can transform it into constructive motivation. When thoughts like *"I can't do this"* arise, we must consciously replace them with *"I am capable and growing stronger every day."* And perhaps most importantly, we must recognize that seeking help is a sign of strength, not weakness. Whether it's therapy, open conversations with loved ones, or simply acknowledging our struggles, healing begins when we allow ourselves to be supported.

The hardest moments in life may shake us, but they also have the power to shape us. The toughest days create the toughest individuals, and that includes you. No matter where you are in your journey, you have the power to reclaim your mind, break through mental barriers, and design a future that aligns with your highest potential. Resilience is not reserved for the lucky, it's built by those who choose to rise, again and again. And that choice is yours to make.

Key notes from the chapter-

1. Struggles Are Temporary, but Resilience Defines Us:
2. Life's challenges may seem overwhelming, but no hardship lasts forever. Building resilience is key to navigating difficulties and emerging stronger.
3. Societal and Digital Pressures Fuel Anxiety:
4. Unrealistic expectations, social media comparisons, and academic/workplace pressures contribute to rising mental health struggles. Emotional well-being should be prioritized over external validation.
5. Emotional Intelligence and Resilience Should Be Taught Early:
6. Schools focus on academics but often neglect teaching emotional resilience and mental well-being. Incorporating mindfulness, stress management, and emotional intelligence into education can better equip individuals for life's challenges.
7. Mindfulness, CBT, and Positive Psychology Help Rewire the Brain:
8. Practices like meditation, Cognitive Behavioral Therapy (CBT), gratitude exercises, and physical well-being can reshape thought patterns, reduce anxiety, and promote emotional balance.
9. The Mind Can Be Reprogrammed for Success:
10. Techniques like the Silva Method, visualization, affirmations, and mental rehearsal allow individuals to shift from limiting beliefs to a growth mindset, unlocking greater confidence and potential.
11. Resilience Is a Skill That Can Be Built:

12. Overcoming adversity isn't about avoiding hardships but learning how to respond to them. Through consistent mental habits, emotional mastery, and seeking support when needed, anyone can strengthen their ability to handle life's ups and downs.

Chapter 6:
From Chaos to Calm- Journey of Healing

As much as we may resist the thought, our past defines us in ways more surreal than we often acknowledge. It lingers in the corners of our minds, shaping our thoughts, influencing our choices, and subtly guiding the way we navigate life. Beyond what we consciously perceive or express, it leaves behind remnants and traces of emotions, lessons, and unspoken fears, woven into the very fabric of our soul and subconscious.

It could be anything, a triumphant victory that instilled confidence, a painful betrayal that built walls around our hearts, or even a seemingly uneventful afternoon that unknowingly altered our perspective. Sometimes, it's the moments we remember vividly that shape us, and other times, it's the ones we barely recall that leave the deepest marks. A passing comment, an unfulfilled promise, an act of kindness, or a disappointment too small to dwell on at the time, all of these contribute to the silent construction of our belief system.

The way we see the world is not merely a reflection of what's in front of us; it is filtered through the lens of where we've been. Our past determines the fears we hold, the trust we give, the love we accept, and even the limits we place upon ourselves, Whether we realize it or not, we carry it with us,.sometimes as a weight, sometimes as wisdom, and always as a part of who we are.

The past has a way of shaping us, bringing out both our best and worst qualities, often depending on how we choose to perceive and internalize the events that shaped us. It's fascinating to think about how every experience, every decision, every fleeting moment we've lived through contributes to who we are today. In many ways, we are nothing more than the sum of what has happened to us and, more importantly, how we react and our response to it.

It's an action-and-reaction kind of conundrum, one that might seem oversimplified at first, yet holds a profound truth. Every triumph, every heartbreak, and every seemingly insignificant event creates ripples that extend far beyond the moment itself. A single act of kindness might shape our ability to trust others, just as one betrayal could lead us to build walls around ourselves. Even those moments we barely remember, the ones that slipped by unnoticed at the time, can still leave traces that shape our beliefs, fears, and ambitions.

This concept mesmerizes me because it highlights the intricate, almost poetic way in which life unfolds. We are not just individuals moving through time; we are walking reflections of our past experiences, constantly evolving as we process and react to them. The way we see the world, the choices we make, the people we let in or push away, all of it stemming from this continuous cycle of cause and effect.

While this might sound deterministic, what makes it truly intriguing is the power of perception. The same event can either break a person or make them stronger, depending on how they interpret it. This chapter will delve deeper into this idea, exploring not just the undeniable influence of our past but also the ways in which we can reshape its impact. Because while we may be products of our experiences, we are not prisoners to them, we have the ability to redefine what they mean to us.

It all comes down to perception and reaction. More often than not, we find ourselves afraid of certain situations, not necessarily because of the situations themselves but because of how they make us feel. In those moments, we experience a loss of control, not just over external circumstances but over our own emotions and senses. Fear, anger, jealousy, grief, and other powerful emotions take hold of us, clouding our judgment and making us feel as though we are at the mercy of what's happening around us. It's in these moments of heightened emotion that we feel most vulnerable, as if we are merely reacting rather than making conscious choices and responding effectively.

But here's the reality, we cannot change what happens to us in life. Tragedies will strike, disappointments will occur, and circumstances beyond our control will unfold in ways we never expected or wanted. Life, by its very nature, is unpredictable and often unfair. However, amidst this unpredictability, there exists one undeniable truth: we have absolute control over how we respond.

This realization is nothing short of a superpower. It is the key to inner peace, to resilience, and ultimately, to a life that is not dictated by external forces but shaped by our own will. The moment we understand that we have the ability to choose our reaction, everything changes. Instead of allowing setbacks to define us, we can choose to see them as lessons. Instead of letting pain consume us, we can choose to grow from it. Instead of succumbing to bitterness, we can choose to seek wisdom.

Imagine the difference between two people who experience the same hardship, one may let it break them, believing life is unfair and retreating into negativity, while the other may see it as an opportunity to evolve, becoming stronger and more compassionate as a result. The event remains the same, but the impact it has is entirely determined by perception and response.

Of course, this is easier said than done. It takes practice, self-awareness, and a willingness to pause before reacting. It requires us to step outside of our immediate emotions and ask ourselves: Is this worth my peace? Can I find a lesson in this? How can I respond in a way that empowers me rather than weakens me? Over time, mastering this ability allows life to flow more smoothly, not because we avoid hardships, but because we no longer allow them to dictate our happiness.

True strength lies not in avoiding pain but in choosing how it shapes us. And once we realize that power is within us, life no longer feels like something happening to us, but something we actively shape through our responses.

This chapter serves as a continuation of the previous one, guiding the reader towards practical solutions for breaking free from destructive patterns and stepping into a life of healing and self-awareness. While acknowledging the influence of the past, this chapter shifts focus toward transformation, how one can consciously reshape their thoughts, emotions, and actions to create a more fulfilling and peaceful existence.

Healing, however, is not a one-size-fits-all process. It is deeply personal, shaped by an individual's experiences, emotional resilience, and willingness to confront their inner wounds. For some, healing might come through self-reflection and meditation; for others, it could require therapy, creative expression, or even significant lifestyle changes. There is no universal timeline, no fixed method; what works for one person may not work for another, and that is entirely okay.

One of the most crucial aspects of healing is resisting the urge to compare one's journey to someone else's. In an age where social media often highlights only the polished, triumphant moments of others, it's easy to feel as though one is falling behind or failing to "heal fast enough." But healing is not a race, nor is it something that can be measured by external standards. Some wounds take longer to mend than others, and forcing progress before one is ready can sometimes do more harm than good.

It's important to approach healing with patience, self-compassion, and an understanding that setbacks are a natural part of the process. Some days will feel lighter, filled with clarity and peace, while others may bring back old wounds and familiar struggles. This ebb and flow is not a sign of failure, it's simply the nature of growth.

Through this chapter, the reader will explore different approaches to breaking free from negative cycles, including mindset shifts, practical self-care techniques, and tools for emotional resilience. More importantly, they will be reminded that no matter how long the journey takes, every step forward, no matter how small, is a victory in itself.

The core aspect of healing involves addressing yourself on multiple levels: mentally, spiritually, and physically. So that you can release past traumas and lingering emotional burdens that have been holding you back. Often, the experiences we go through shape our self-perception, leading to self-limiting beliefs that make us doubt our worth, capabilities, and potential. These beliefs can stem from pain, rejection, failure, or loss, and if left unaddressed, they silently dictate our decisions, relationships, and the way we view the world.

The first and most crucial step in healing is making peace with what happened, not by justifying or diminishing the pain but by accepting that the past cannot be changed. Many of us spend years replaying old events, wondering what if or blaming ourselves or others, only to realize that no amount of mental resistance can undo what has already occurred. True healing begins when we acknowledge that circumstances, especially painful ones, are often beyond our control, but our response to them is always within our power. Life does not have to be perfect or predictable to be meaningful and beautiful; in fact, the very struggles we face add depth, resilience, and wisdom to our existence. The ups and downs, the heartbreaks and breakthroughs, all contribute to the richness of our journey.

When we choose to heal and move forward, we create space for something incredibly powerful, the ability to redefine how we react to challenges. Rather than being stuck in cycles of pain, anger, or regret, we cultivate the emotional freedom to respond with clarity, wisdom, and grace. This transformation makes us more grounded, emotionally stable, and in touch with our inner world, allowing us to break free from old patterns and live with greater intention. Healing is not about erasing the past, it is about learning from it, reshaping its impact, and stepping into a version of ourselves that is not defined by pain, but by strength and self-awareness.

Spiritual healing is a deeply personal and transformative journey that allows us to reconnect with our inner selves and release the emotional burdens we carry. One of the most profound ways to heal spiritually is through meditation, which helps quiet the mind, bring awareness to the present moment, and create space for self-reflection. Practices such as mindfulness meditation, loving-kindness meditation, guided visualization, and breathwork can all aid in emotional release and clarity. In addition to meditation, somatic work focuses on healing through the body, as trauma and emotions often get stored within our muscles and nervous system. Yoga, breathwork, dance therapy, and body scanning techniques help in releasing pent-up energy and restoring balance between the mind and body.

Another powerful way to heal from within is through rituals that bring intention and mindfulness into daily life. Journaling can serve as a form of emotional release, while energy-cleansing practices such as smudging with sage help remove stagnant energy. Sound healing through singing bowls, chanting, or listening to calming frequencies helps realign energy, while affirmations and gratitude practices shift the subconscious mind toward healing and positivity. The key to spiritual healing is finding what resonates most with you, whether it's stillness, movement, or intentional rituals. By embracing these practices, healing becomes more than just overcoming the past; it becomes a sacred journey of self-discovery, emotional liberation, and inner peace.

Traumas and personal struggles often serve as invisible weights on our souls, subtly shaping our thoughts, emotions, and decisions. Just as trying to run with heavy baggage makes it more challenging to move toward our goals and dreams, being burdened by emotional wounds complicates our journey.

Healing is not just about overcoming pain; it is about freeing ourselves from what no longer serves us so that we can move forward with clarity and purpose. When we heal, we strip away the self-doubt, negative thought patterns, and limiting beliefs that have kept us stuck. This not only accelerates personal growth but also allows us to step into our fullest potential, mentally, emotionally, and spiritually. Without the heaviness of past wounds clouding our vision, we can set intentions with confidence, pursue our dreams without fear, and open ourselves up to joy, love, and new opportunities.

To facilitate this, it is essential to build a healthy and nurturing relationship with oneself, one based on self-awareness, self-compassion, and deep inner trust. True growth happens when we align the mind, body, and soul, creating harmony between our thoughts, emotions, and actions. This means being mindful of our mental well-being, taking care of our physical health, and nourishing our spiritual self in a way that feels authentic to us. Healing is not about erasing the past; it is about transforming our relationship with it. When we make peace with our experiences and embrace our journey, we not only grow stronger but also gain the wisdom and resilience needed to create a life that feels truly fulfilling.

In addition, I would like to share something close to my heart, Reiki healing. As a certified Reiki healer, I've had the privilege of witnessing its gentle yet profound impact on energy and well-being. Introduced to me by a dear friend, Reiki opened my eyes to the transformative potential of channeling universal energy through intention and compassion. While it may sound mystical, with talk of energy, chakras, and the power of love, it is an experience that speaks louder than words. I wholeheartedly invite my readers to explore this beautiful practice for themselves.

Reiki is a gentle yet profound energy healing technique that has been practiced for centuries. Rooted in the belief that all living beings possess a vital life force, it aims to restore balance, promote healing, and enhance overall well-being. It is a holistic practice that integrates physical, emotional, and spiritual healing, making it an effective alternative therapy for those seeking peace, clarity, and vitality in their lives. In my personal experience, Reiki has been a transformative force, offering me a deeper understanding of the power of positive thinking, gratitude, and love. Reiki has shown that true healing goes beyond merely treating symptoms, it's about identifying and addressing the root cause of imbalances within our energy fields. Many who have embraced this practice report a growing sense of harmony between mind, body, and soul. As a certified Reiki healer, I've observed how consistent practice can foster this alignment, offering a path toward deeper well-being that anyone can benefit from.

Reiki, which translates to "universal life energy," is a form of alternative healing where the practitioner channels energy into the recipient through their hands. The goal is to remove blockages, enhance energy flow, and facilitate self-healing. The practice is based on the idea that when energy becomes stagnant or unbalanced due to stress, trauma, or negative emotions, it can lead to physical or emotional ailments. By restoring the natural flow of energy, Reiki promotes relaxation, reduces pain, and encourages deep healing. Reiki was developed in the early 20th century by Mikao Usui, a Japanese Buddhist monk. Usui's teachings emphasized that Reiki is not just a healing technique but also a way of life. The practice is guided by five principles that encourage practitioners to cultivate inner peace and mindfulness: Just for today, I will not be angry. Just for today, I will not worry. Just for today, I will be grateful. Just for today, I will do my work honestly. Just for today, I will be kind to every living thing. These principles serve as a foundation for a balanced and harmonious life, reinforcing the idea that healing begins with a shift in mindset and attitude.

Reiki sessions typically involve the recipient lying down in a relaxed state while the practitioner places their hands lightly on or just above different energy centers of the body. The practitioner then channels healing energy, allowing it to flow through the recipient's body and remove any blockages or imbalances. Many people describe the experience as deeply calming, with sensations of warmth, tingling, or gentle waves of energy moving through their bodies. A Reiki session usually lasts between 45 to 90 minutes. The process is completely non-invasive, requiring no physical manipulation, medication, or medical intervention. Instead, it focuses on harnessing the universal energy that is available to all of us. While some people experience immediate benefits, others may notice subtle shifts over time as their body and mind adjust to the renewed flow of energy. Reiki can also be channeled to yourself, from and for yourself, called self healing.

Through my own practice, I have witnessed the profound impact Reiki can have on various aspects of life. Some of the key benefits of Reiki include physical healing and pain relief. Reiki is often used to alleviate physical discomfort, reduce inflammation, and support the body's natural healing processes. It has been reported to help with chronic pain, migraines, digestive issues, and even recovery from surgery. By restoring balance in the body's energy field, Reiki allows the body to heal itself more efficiently. One of the most powerful aspects of Reiki is its ability to soothe emotional distress. Many people carry unresolved emotions, past traumas, or daily stress that manifest in anxiety, depression, or emotional blockages. Reiki helps release these suppressed emotions, bringing a sense of clarity, inner peace, and emotional stability. It encourages positive thinking, allowing individuals to shift from a place of fear and worry to gratitude and acceptance. In our fast-paced world, stress has become a common factor in most people's lives. Reiki induces a state of deep relaxation, slowing down the nervous system and promoting a feeling of calm. It helps release tension, quiet the mind, and reduce cortisol levels, making it an effective tool for managing stress-related conditions.

Reiki is not just about physical and emotional healing, it also opens the door to spiritual growth. It encourages self-awareness, deepens intuition, and enhances one's connection with the universe. Many individuals find that regular Reiki practice helps them align with their higher purpose, uncover hidden strengths, and experience a greater sense of fulfillment in life. Reiki teaches us the power of love, kindness, and gratitude. By healing ourselves, we also improve our interactions with others. Reiki fosters compassion and understanding, helping us let go of resentment, anger, and negativity. When we operate from a place of love and inner peace, our relationships become healthier and more harmonious.

A close friend once shared how they had long struggled with emotional baggage and limiting beliefs that seemed to shadow every step forward. Despite trying to maintain a positive mindset, they often found themselves entangled in self-doubt, anxiety, and moments of unworthiness. Their transformation after discovering Reiki was profound, and witnessing their journey firsthand is what inspired me to explore the practice more deeply and eventually become a certified Reiki healer.It wasn't until I experienced Reiki firsthand that I truly understood the power of energy healing. During my first session, I remember feeling a deep warmth and sensation of energy flowing through my body. By the end of the session, I felt lighter, as though a weight had been lifted from my soul. Over time, as I continued receiving Reiki and eventually learned how to practice it myself, I noticed profound shifts in my emotional resilience, stress levels, and overall well-being. The practice taught me that healing is a journey, not a destination. It showed me that while we cannot control everything that happens in life, we can control how we respond to it. By embracing positive thinking, gratitude, and self-love, I was able to release old wounds and step into a more empowered version of myself.

If you are new to Reiki, there are several ways to incorporate its healing energy into your daily routine: Schedule a Reiki session with a certified practitioner to experience its benefits firsthand. Practice self-Reiki and learn the basics of Reiki to channel healing energy for yourself. Use affirmations and gratitude to combine Reiki with positive affirmations and gratitude journaling to shift your mindset. Meditate with Reiki and use Reiki energy during meditation to enhance relaxation and inner connection. Share Reiki with others, as once attuned, you can offer Reiki to loved ones, pets, and even plants. It is a gentle yet powerful healing practice that offers profound benefits for the mind, body, and soul. Whether you are seeking relief from stress, emotional healing, or spiritual growth, Reiki provides a pathway to greater harmony and self-discovery. The journey with Reiki can be one of profound transformation, as many practitioners and recipients have experienced, allowing me and other practitioners to cultivate peace, gratitude, and love in ways I never imagined. If you are open to exploring energy healing, I highly recommend giving Reiki a try, it just might be the key to unlocking your inner balance and well-being.

Healing from childhood trauma is not about forgetting the past, it is about freeing yourself from its grip. It is about recognizing that while your experiences have shaped you, they do not have to define you. The pain, the fear, the moments of despair, they were chapters in your story, but they are not the whole book.

True healing happens when you stop carrying your wounds as a burden and start wearing them as wisdom. It happens when you choose to honor your past, not as a prison but as proof of your strength. It is the realization that every scar is a testament to survival, every setback a lesson, and every painful memory an opportunity for growth.

Mentally, healing means reshaping the narratives you tell yourself. It is replacing self-doubt with self-belief, fear with courage, and sorrow with hope. It is learning that your worth is not defined by what happened to you but by how you rise beyond it.

Physically, healing means reclaiming your body as a temple of strength rather than a vessel of pain. It means treating yourself with care, honoring your well-being, and understanding that your body deserves love, movement, and nourishment, just as much as your soul does.

Spiritually, healing is the art of letting go. It is the realization that you are not bound by the suffering of yesterday. It is learning to trust the universe, to surrender the weight of what was, and to step forward into what can be. It is understanding that your spirit is unbreakable, even when life has tried to shatter it.

The past is a place of reference, not a place of residence. It is part of your journey, but it is not your final destination. As you turn this page, know that you are stepping into a new chapter, one where you are not a victim of your past but the author of your future.

And this time, you get to write the story on your own terms.

Key notes from the chapter-

1. Healing is about self-awareness, not fixing yourself.
2. You are not broken. Healing involves recognizing and releasing layers of emotional and mental conditioning.
3. Emotions are indicators, not problems.

4. Triggers and emotional pain highlight areas that need attention and healing and not suppression.
5. Softness is strength.
6. Vulnerability and emotional openness are essential for genuine healing and inner growth.
7. Inner child work is crucial.
8. Many adult behaviors stem from unmet childhood needs. Re-parenting your inner child fosters emotional stability.
9. Energy healing supports deep transformation.
10. Techniques like Reiki help release stored emotional energy and restore balance at the energetic level.
11. You are your primary healer.
12. Healing is an internal process. External tools can guide, but true change comes from within.

Chapter 7:
Attracting Abundance with Gratitude.

Late at night, after long days of rejection and auditions that went nowhere, Jim Carrey would drive up into the hills above the city. He'd park his car on Mulholland Drive, look out over the lights of Los Angeles, and imagine a different life. Not in a vague and wishful way, but in detail. He saw himself being offered roles, walking onto sets, cashing big checks. He didn't just hope for it. He saw it. And then, in one of those moments where an idea feels more like an instruction, he took out his checkbook and wrote himself a check: Ten million dollars for his acting services. He dated it Thanksgiving 1995, folded it, and put it in his wallet.

That check stayed with him for years, through countless setbacks, frustrations, and uncertain months where nothing seemed to be happening.But he kept showing up. Kept performing. Kept believing, and just before Thanksgiving of 1995, Carrey landed a deal to star in Dumb and Dumber, a role that came with a paycheck for exactly ten million dollars. The same number he had written down years earlier, when it made absolutely no sense at all.

Before Jim Carrey became one of the most recognizable names in Hollywood, he was just another struggling comedian in Los Angeles. He had no major credits, no big roles lined up, and barely enough money to get by. But what he did have was a strange kind of conviction, not quite arrogance, not quite blind optimism, but a focused belief that success wasn't just possible, it was inevitable. Now, he's one of the most successful actors Hollywood has ever seen, bagging multiple roles in blockbusters such as The Mask,

The Truman Show, and Eternal Sunshine. He's a two-time Golden Globe winner, known for blending wild comedy with deep emotional range. Beyond acting, he's also an artist, writer, and outspoken voice on manifestation, creativity, and consciousness. Later, Carrey would say that visualization alone isn't enough. "You can't just visualize and then go eat a sandwich," he said. It's not about fantasy, it's about alignment. You imagine it, yes. But then you do the work. You build the habits. You stay committed long enough for reality to meet you halfway.

What makes his story powerful isn't just that it came true, it's when he chose to believe it. At a time when things were not working out, there was no proof or guarantee of his cheque coming to reality, no backup plan, nothing but a check in his wallet and a future he chose to believe in anyway. Most people wait for evidence before they commit to a vision. Jim Carrey did the opposite. He committed first, and the evidence came later.

Following up on Chapter 7, we now move beyond concepts and dive into the lived experience of aligning your energy with your desires. At the heart of this transformation lie two core elements: gratitude and manifestation. Though often spoken of as separate practices, they are, in reality, deeply entwined. Gratitude is not simply an emotion or an act of politeness, it is an energetic declaration to the universe that says, "I recognize abundance, and I am ready to receive more." Manifestation, then, is the unfolding of that energetic alignment into reality. When practiced together, these two form the foundation of a powerful and intentional life.

This alignment becomes even more potent when brought into the context of Reiki, a gentle but profound energy healing technique that taps into universal life force. Reiki works like an amplifier. It clears emotional and energetic blockages, making space for gratitude to settle deeper and for intentions to root stronger. When you send Reiki to a desire, you're not trying to control the outcome; you're offering it the purest frequency of love, trust, and readiness. It's about creating a container in which your manifestation can safely bloom. Through daily Reiki self-treatment, you start nurturing the soil of your subconscious, making it fertile for your intentions to thrive.

Gratitude, when felt deeply and consistently, naturally lifts your vibration. And it is this frequency, high, open, and receptive, that calls in what you seek. Many people attempt manifestation from a place of lack or desperation. They focus on what's missing. But when gratitude becomes your baseline, you start manifesting not from fear, but from fullness. You begin to operate from a reality where you already feel abundant, safe, and supported. This is where tools like mirror work and affirmations become more than just exercises, they become ways to rewire your inner dialogue to match the frequency of your desires. It's no longer about hoping to believe; it's about becoming what you already are inside.

Mirror work, a method popularized by Louise Hay, is not merely about speaking affirmations into a mirror. It's about coming face to face with yourself and challenging the old stories that have shaped your self-worth. When you say, "I am worthy of abundance" while looking into your own eyes, you're not just hoping to convince yourself, you're speaking to the parts of you that have long been waiting to hear it. This vulnerability, this willingness to stand with yourself, is powerful. And when combined with Reiki, your hands gently placed over your heart as you speak, it creates a deep, cellular kind of healing that words alone can't reach. This layered practice builds new neural pathways and emotional memories, replacing past conditioning with a new energetic truth.

Affirmations, journaling, and vision boards are not separate acts, either. They are extensions of this internal reprogramming. Affirmations are the language of your new vibration, repeated not to trick the mind, but to realign it. A well-crafted affirmation feels like a remembered truth rather than a forced statement. Writing them down in a journal, alongside expressions of gratitude, transforms fleeting thoughts into declarations. Your journal becomes a sacred container, holding both what you've received and what you're calling in. This consistent recording of evidence helps retrain your perception to spot synchronicities, reinforcing belief in the unseen.

Journaling can take many forms. Sometimes, it's scripting-a method where you write about your life as if your dreams have already come true. This act moves your vision from concept into felt experience. Other times, it's shadow work, exploring the beliefs and fears that sabotage your growth. When you write through resistance, with your hand resting on a Reiki-charged crystal or simply after a moment of deep breathing, you allow the truth to flow through without judgment. Reiki, again, can hold space during these practices, helping to calm the nervous system and allow truth to rise without resistance. Lighting a candle, channeling energy into your hands, and writing from the heart, this is not just journaling, its also a ritual. And rituals, when repeated with intent, become anchors in your transformational journey.

Then there is the vision board. Not just a collage of dreams, but a visual affirmation of your new identity. Every image you place on it should spark recognition, not just of what you want, but of who you are becoming. When you look at it daily, especially after a gratitude practice or during a

Reiki session, you're reinforcing this identity. You're reminding your subconscious, "This is my path." And because the subconscious mind speaks in symbols and emotion, the vision board communicates in the language it understands best. More than a tool of visualization, it becomes a symbol of trust, a beacon of your unfolding reality.

All these practices, when layered together, create a field of coherence. You begin your day with mirror work, speaking to yourself as the empowered version of you. You follow it with a brief Reiki self-treatment, balancing your energy and setting intentions with love. You journal not just what you're grateful for now, but what you're already thankful for in your unfolding future. You revisit your vision board, not as a wish list, but as a reflection of your truth. None of these practices are isolated. They form a loop, a cycle of energetic coherence that grounds you in presence while pulling you toward possibility.

Over time, this integration does more than align your energy, it transforms how you perceive and interact with the world. You begin to recognize signs and synchronicities as confirmations rather than coincidences. You notice how the right people, opportunities, and messages begin to flow your way. You become attuned to inspired action, the natural steps that arise when your energy and intention are in harmony. And most importantly, you no longer feel separate from your desires. You realize that everything you are calling in is already part of you, waiting to be uncovered.

In truth, manifestation is not about controlling life, it's about becoming so aligned with your vision that reality has no choice but to meet you there. Gratitude makes that vision fertile. Reiki nurtures it. Your words, your images, your rituals, they are all tools of remembrance. You are not becoming something new. You are remembering what was always possible. The energy, the worth, the readiness, it's already within you.

Let this integration be your path. Let it be gentle, but consistent. Let each practice reinforce the next, like pieces of a puzzle locking into place. In doing so, you stop chasing your dreams and start embodying them. You move from hoping, to knowing. From striving, to receiving. And from waiting, to living.

Manifestation is more than often misunderstood as a passive process, a daydream, a wish, or a vision board stuck to the wall. But those who have experienced true, lasting transformation know it is much more. Manifestation is not just writing about your desired future or repeating affirmations into the mirror. It's not merely talking about what you want. While those steps are important, they are the first ripple in a much deeper current. Real manifestation requires alignment, of thought, energy, and most crucially, action.

Thoughts and intentions lay the groundwork. They shape the vision, clarify your desires, and begin the process of energetic alignment. But without action, they remain potential energy, ideas floating in the ether, waiting for substance. Manifestation happens in the space where inner alignment meets outward behavior. It is in the consistent, embodied actions that you begin to shape reality around your desires.

This doesn't always mean taking massive leaps. In fact, the most powerful manifestations often come from small, conscious, and deliberate steps. These are the choices that reflect a belief in your vision, even before it materializes. For example, if you're manifesting a new career, aligned action might look like updating your resume, networking with people in your desired field, taking a course to refine your skills, or waking up earlier to dedicate time to that goal. These actions signal to your subconscious, and to the universe, that you are serious. That you're not just wishing, you're preparing.

The subconscious mind plays a critical role in manifestation. It governs over 90% of our daily thoughts, behaviors, and reactions. When we engage in intentional rituals like mirror work, affirmations, journaling, or vision boarding, we're not just playing with inspiration, we're actively reprogramming our subconscious. These tools start shifting the internal narrative. But the shift solidifies when our behavior begins to echo the new story.

Every action you take either reinforces your old story or builds your new one. If your inner affirmation is "I am worthy of abundance," yet you consistently say yes to underpaid work or avoid financial planning, there's a disconnect. On the other hand, when your actions reflect your affirmation, by advocating for better pay, budgeting with clarity, or investing in your growth, you begin to manifest in motion. Your subconscious sees evidence that the belief is not only possible, but already active.

Some forms of action are more subtle. Cleaning your home, organizing your schedule, or clearing physical and digital clutter are all energetic acts of preparation. You're making room. This sends a powerful message: I am ready. Similarly, taking care of your body, setting boundaries in relationships, or prioritizing rest can also be forms of manifestation. They reflect a belief in your worthiness and capacity to receive. These are subconscious cues that build momentum, even if you don't see immediate results.

Then there's inspired action, the intuitive nudge, the gut feeling that tells you to send that email, show up to that event, or start that passion project. These are often the breadcrumbs the universe lays in your path. When you follow them, not out of fear or desperation, but from a place of curiosity and trust, you activate co-creation. You show up to meet the universe halfway. And often, this is where the most magical synchronicities unfold.

Remember, manifestation is not about controlling every step of the outcome. It's about becoming a vibrational match to what you desire and letting your life reflect that match. It's living as though the dream is already true, even if the evidence hasn't fully arrived yet. And the beauty is, when your actions, words, thoughts, and energy all speak the same language, the world starts to respond in kind.

In the end, manifestation isn't a spell or a shortcut. It's a relationship with your own potential. It asks for your vision, your belief, and your effort. It invites you to show up again and again, with faith in what you can't yet see, and with the courage to move in its direction anyway. That is where real transformation lives, not in the wish, but in the walk.

Gratitude is often mistaken for a simple expression of politeness, something we say out of habit, like a simple "thank you". But in truth, gratitude is one of the most transformative mindsets we can cultivate. It is the quiet force that helps us shift our focus from what's lacking to what is present and abundant. When we choose to be grateful, even in the face of challenges, we train our minds to see life through a lens of possibility rather than scarcity. This shift in perspective is not just comforting; it is empowering. Gratitude softens the harshness of our inner dialogue, replacing complaint with appreciation, and restlessness with peace.

On a mental and emotional level, gratitude acts as a powerful stabilizer. Scientific studies consistently show that those who regularly practice gratitude experience reduced levels of anxiety, depression, and stress. They sleep better, have higher self-esteem, and are more optimistic about the future. it's mindset, the attitude of gratitude. By focusing on what's working, what's beautiful, and what's meaningful, we create an internal environment that supports growth and well-being. The habit doesn't erase our problems, but it gives us the strength to face them with clarity and resilience.

Spiritually, gratitude is a doorway to presence. When we pause to appreciate a moment, a breath of fresh air, a smile from a loved one, or the silence of a sunrise, we connect to something greater than ourselves. This awareness deepens our sense of peace and purpose. In many ancient traditions, gratitude is considered a sacred act, an offering to the divine. It's a way of saying, "I see the gifts, even in the chaos." This simple awareness transforms everyday experiences into spiritual ones, grounding us in humility and openness.

Gratitude also strengthens our relationships. When we express appreciation for the people around us, we invite connection and trust. We shift from taking to acknowledging, from expecting to valuing. Whether in personal or professional settings, people thrive when they feel seen and appreciated. A heartfelt "thank you" can mend wounds, deepen bonds, and build lasting loyalty. Gratitude, when genuine, has the power to heal not just our own hearts but the hearts of those around us.

Perhaps most remarkably, gratitude lays the foundation for lasting success. While ambition drives us forward, gratitude keeps us grounded. It reminds us to celebrate the small wins and learn from setbacks. When we recognize how far we've come and appreciate what we already have, we create the emotional fuel needed to keep going. Gratitude increases motivation, enhances creativity, and invites new opportunities. It shifts our energy from desperation to confidence, from lack to abundance. In this state, we become more open, more receptive, and more aligned with the flow of life.

The beauty of gratitude lies in its simplicity. It requires no special tools or perfect conditions, just a willing heart and a bit of awareness. Whether through a journal, a morning reflection, or a few quiet words spoken before sleep, the act of acknowledging what is good creates ripples that extend far beyond the moment. Gratitude, when practiced consistently, becomes more than a habit; it becomes a way of life. A quiet superpower. A daily anchor. And a steady reminder that even in the midst of uncertainty, we are already surrounded by more blessings than we often realize.

Gratitude has long been celebrated in philosophical and spiritual traditions, but only in recent decades has empirical research begun to unpack its measurable impact on psychological well-being. A series of studies, cited in a paper on pubmed by Emmons and McCullough provided some of the earliest experimental evidence supporting this connection. Participants in their study were randomly assigned to one of three journaling conditions: one group recorded daily hassles or negative events, another listed things for which they were grateful, and a third noted neutral life events. The results were consistent across various iterations of the experiment- those who engaged in gratitude journaling reported significantly higher levels of well-being, including more optimism, greater satisfaction with life, and fewer physical symptoms. Gratitude, it seemed, was not just a pleasant emotion but a cognitive practice capable of shifting one's entire psychological orientation.

Building on this foundation, Dickerhoof conducted an experiment designed to equalize participant expectations about the outcome, thereby reducing placebo effects. Students were told that either of the two experimental exercises could enhance well-being. One group engaged in a "happiness paradigm," which included writing about their best possible future selves (manifestation, simply put) or composing letters of gratitude. The control group, in contrast, simply wrote about events from the past week. The findings reinforced previous research: the happiness-oriented exercises, particularly those involving gratitude, led to measurable increases in well-being, suggesting that gratitude can catalyze positive psychological change even when the participants are unaware of its specific benefits.

The power of gratitude is not limited to adults. Froh et al. extended this inquiry to adolescents in a study involving 221 participants. The students were divided into three groups: one practiced a gratitude exercise (listing blessings), another focused on daily irritants, and the third engaged in a neutral task. As anticipated, the gratitude group experienced a significant boost in life satisfaction. What's particularly striking is that this effect was observed during adolescence, a developmental stage often characterized by emotional turbulence. The implication is that gratitude can serve as a stabilizing psychological anchor even during periods of heightened emotional flux.

Finally, Wood and colleagues explored the relationship between gratitude and personality, examining a sample of 389 adults. Their findings revealed that gratitude is not only positively associated with well-being but also uniquely predictive of it, beyond the effects of other personality traits such as extraversion or neuroticism. In other words, gratitude is not simply a byproduct of a cheerful disposition, it contributes something distinct to a person's overall life satisfaction.

Together, these studies provide robust support for the transformative power of gratitude. It is not merely a social virtue or an abstract ideal; it is a practical, evidence-based intervention that can enhance mental health, foster resilience, and improve quality of life across diverse populations. Far from being sentimental or simplistic, gratitude emerges from the data as a serious and effective tool for cultivating psychological well-being.

As we close this chapter, let this truth settle into your heart: you do not chase abundance, you become it. The journey to manifesting your desires is not about forcing outcomes or wishing harder. It is about aligning your energy with the life you envision, embodying your intentions with clarity, and stepping into the version of yourself who already lives that reality.

Whether it's through Reiki healing, the quiet power of mirror work, the daily commitment to affirmations, or the visualization of your dreams on a vision board, every practice you engage in becomes a mirror of your inner world. And that inner world, shaped by gratitude, belief, and conscious intention, is what ultimately reflects back into your reality.

Gratitude remains the thread that weaves it all together. It grounds your energy in what is already working, anchoring you in the present while opening your heart to receive more. When you live in gratitude, you shift from lack to sufficiency, from waiting to creating. You stop asking life to give you more, and instead, you begin to radiate more, attracting what you desire by becoming a vibrational match for it.

Abundance is not a distant reward; it is a state of being. It is cultivated from within through your thoughts, your emotions, your habits, and most importantly, your self-image. When you believe you are worthy, when you speak life into your dreams, and when you nurture your spirit with loving practices, the universe responds in kind.

You are the creator. The mirror. The magnet. The masterpiece in motion.

So, take a deep breath, stand tall in front of your mirror, and begin to affirm the truth: "I am abundant. I am enough. I am becoming all that I am meant to be." Let this become your daily ritual, your energetic signature, your sacred promise to yourself. Because in the end, attracting abundance isn't about having more, it's about being more of who you truly are.

And that version of you? They are already waiting on the other side of belief.

Key notes from the chapter-

1. Jim Carrey's Manifestation Story: Jim Carrey wrote himself a check for $10 million during a tough time, visualized his success, and years later, landed a role that paid exactly that amount, demonstrating the power of belief and vision.

2. Manifestation is More Than Visualization: True manifestation requires aligning energy with desire, combining gratitude, intention, and action. It's not just about wishing; it's about clearing blockages and taking steps toward your goals.

3. Gratitude Enhances Manifestation: Gratitude isn't just an emotion; it's an energetic declaration of abundance. When paired with Reiki, it clears energetic blockages and helps you connect deeply with your desires, paving the way for transformation.

4. Tools for Alignment: Practices like mirror work, affirmations, journaling, and vision boards help shift your subconscious beliefs and align your energy with your desires, supporting your manifestation process.

5. Action is Key: Manifestation requires intentional action. Visualization and affirmations are important, but taking concrete steps,like updating a resume or committing to growth signals seriousness and attracts opportunities.

6. You Are the Creator of Your Reality: By aligning your thoughts, energy, and actions with your desires, you become a vibrational match for them. Abundance isn't something you seek,it's something you become.

Chapter 8:
The Power of Meditation and Spirituality

Spiritual practices have been central to human life for thousands of years, offering tools for peace, healing, clarity, and a deeper connection to ourselves and the world around us. From ancient rituals under open skies to modern mindfulness apps, the path of spirituality has evolved, but its purpose remains rooted in elevating human experience and consciousness.

Spirituality, in its earliest forms, was intertwined with nature and the rhythms of life. Ancient humans honored the elements, the moon cycles, and celestial patterns, believing the world was alive with spirit. Animism- the belief that everything has a soul- formed the spiritual foundation for many early societies.

As civilizations developed, structured religions emerged, each bringing new interpretations and systems of belief. All faiths, especially originating from the east, provided frameworks for spiritual exploration and ethical living. Despite theological differences, these traditions emphasized inner transformation, service, devotion, and transcendence.

In recent decades, we've witnessed a spiritual shift. More people are stepping beyond traditional religious structures and turning inward, seeking direct experience through meditation, mindfulness, energy healing, and self-inquiry . This movement is about rediscovering the inner self and aligning with universal truths that complement and enrich one's personal path, whether rooted in tradition, spirituality, or individual belief.This evolution of spirituality reflects humanity's ongoing quest for meaning, connection, and healing. It's a return to essence, with ancient wisdom meeting modern awareness.

You must be wondering, why does spirituality have an entire chapter devoted to it in this book? It's simply because it is an essential part of our humanity. Spirituality holds a fundamental place in the human experience, not merely as a personal journey but as a shared thread that binds us to our roots, to each other, and to something far greater than ourselves. As I write this, I want you to pause for a moment. Breathe. Feel. Amidst the chaos of deadlines, digital noise, and endless to-do lists, have you felt that gentle nudge from within? That quiet, almost whisper-like pull toward something deeper? That's the beginning of your inner world calling, and that's where spirituality begins.

Throughout history, across every culture and tradition, humans have turned to spiritual practices to understand their place in the universe. These weren't just rituals or routines, they were lifelines to meaning, belonging, and truth. In today's hyper-connected, fast-moving world, spirituality may feel like a luxury or an afterthought. But I promise you, it's more relevant now than ever. It invites us to slow down and tune into what truly matters, not what the world demands from us, but what our soul is longing to express.

Spirituality teaches us compassion, empathy, and the profound realization that we are all connected. These aren't just lofty ideals; they are essential qualities for creating a more loving, peaceful, and sustainable world. Studies from institutions like UC Berkeley's Greater Good Science Center confirm what ancient wisdom has always known: when we practice presence, meditation, prayer, or simply mindful living, our capacity for empathy and kindness expands. We become more human, more attuned not only to our own needs but to the pain and beauty in others.

And here's the thing: life will challenge you. There will be moments of heartbreak, uncertainty, and grief. During those times, spirituality isn't just comforting, it's transformative. It becomes the ground beneath your feet when the world feels like it's crumbling. Research supports this, too; spiritual practices help people process trauma, cope with illness, and find light in the darkest places. They remind us that we're never truly alone, that even in our suffering, there's wisdom and growth waiting to unfold.

As you begin to explore your own spiritual path, or deepen the one you're already on, you'll notice something extraordinary: the inner work you do begins to ripple outward. You make more conscious choices. Your relationships become richer. Your actions start to align with your values. This isn't about perfection; it's about presence. People who are spiritually connected tend to live with intention. And that intentionality changes the world, one mindful decision at a time.

There's even research to back this up. Studies in The Journal of Positive Psychology show that spiritual individuals report higher levels of gratitude, satisfaction, and a desire to serve others. They don't just live for themselves, they live from a place of deeper purpose. And in a world that often feels fragmented and divided, that kind of soulful living is a powerful act of healing.

So why does spirituality matter? Because it reminds us of who we really are beneath the noise. It connects us to the sacred in the everyday. It invites us to see life not just as a series of tasks, but as a journey of discovery, connection, and becoming. And as your fellow traveler on this path, I encourage you: don't ignore that quiet whisper inside.

Follow it. Explore it. Trust it. Because within you lies a world more vast, beautiful, and wise than you've ever imagined, and spirituality is the key that unlocks the door.

At the heart of every spiritual journey lies a few powerful practices that serves as both anchor and guide, one of them being meditation. It is through meditation that we begin to quiet the chatter of the mind and open the doorway to the soul. While spirituality invites us to explore life's deeper meaning and our connection to something greater, meditation offers the practical path to get there.

Meditation is a core spiritual practice found in nearly every tradition, from Vedic chants and Buddhist mindfulness. Science is now catching up to what sages have known for centuries: meditation works.

The practice offers a wide range of benefits that are both scientifically validated and experientially profound. One of the most significant advantages is its ability to reduce stress. Regular meditation practice lowers cortisol levels, which is the primary hormone associated with stress. When cortisol levels drop, the nervous system relaxes, the heart rate stabilizes, and the body shifts from a fight-or-flight mode into a state of rest and recovery. This physiological response not only calms the mind but also has a positive ripple effect on overall health, reducing the risk of stress-related illnesses such as high blood pressure, anxiety, and burnout.

Beyond physical stress reduction, meditation profoundly enhances emotional well-being. It encourages emotional resilience, making it easier to navigate life's ups and downs with a sense of inner stability. Studies have shown that consistent meditation can reduce symptoms of depression and anxiety, contributing to an overall more balanced and positive mood. By creating space between stimulus and response, individuals become less reactive and more mindful in their emotional responses, cultivating a deeper sense of inner peace.

Another powerful benefit of meditation is the development of self-awareness. As individuals sit in stillness and observe their thoughts without judgment, they begin to see patterns in their thinking and behavior. This heightened awareness fosters personal insight and growth, helping people understand the root causes of their emotions and reactions. Over time, this practice can lead to profound inner transformation, as one becomes more aligned with their authentic self and values.

Meditation also sharpens the mind, enhancing focus and attention. In an age where distractions are constant and multitasking is the norm, meditation serves as mental training that improves cognitive function. Practitioners often report an increased ability to concentrate, make decisions with clarity, and remain present in both personal and professional environments. This improved attention span directly supports productivity and mental clarity.

In addition, meditation can greatly enhance sleep quality. By quieting the mind before bedtime, it becomes easier to fall asleep and stay asleep. Meditation helps release the mental chatter and tension that often interferes with rest, promoting a deeper, more restorative sleep cycle. As a result, individuals wake up feeling more refreshed, energized, and ready to engage with the day.

Finally, meditation opens the door to a deeper spiritual connection. Whether one approaches it from a religious, spiritual, or purely introspective angle, meditation creates space to connect with a higher consciousness or inner guidance. This connection often brings a sense of purpose, inner peace, and alignment with something greater than oneself. For many, this aspect of meditation is what transforms it from a daily habit into a meaningful spiritual journey.

In essence, meditation is a powerful tool that supports physical health, emotional balance, mental clarity, and spiritual depth. When practiced consistently, it becomes not just a technique but a way of being, one that nurtures a more peaceful, aware, and fulfilling life.

As you walk the spiritual path, you'll find that meditation is not a one-size-fits-all practice, it's a diverse, evolving discipline with ancient roots and universal reach. Across cultures and centuries, people have turned inward through various forms of meditation to touch the essence of who they truly are. These practices serve as sacred tools, gently peeling back the layers of conditioning, fear, and ego to reveal the radiant self that has always existed within: whole, awakened, and aligned. Meditation, in its many forms, opens us to the possibility of self-actualization, the complete realization and embodiment of our highest potential.

In ancient India, some of the deepest meditative traditions were born, and their impact continues to ripple through time. Take Vipassana, for instance, a profound method that teaches us to observe reality as it is. Rooted in the teachings of the Buddha, Vipassana sharpens awareness of the body's sensations and the mind's movements without judgment. As we observe the transient nature of all experiences, we begin to unhook from our attachments and reactions. With sustained practice, this leads to a liberating insight: we are not our thoughts, emotions, or sensations, we are the one observing them. Through Vipassana, we begin to respond to life with greater clarity, equanimity, and inner freedom.

Then there is Yoga Nidra, often referred to as yogic sleep, a deeply restorative practice where the body enters a sleep-like state while the mind remains consciously aware. This meditative state allows the practitioner to access the subconscious and plant intentions at a level where they can truly take root. Healing happens here, not just physically, but emotionally and spiritually. By journeying inward and resting the nervous system, we begin to release deeply held patterns of fear, shame, or unworthiness. The silence of Yoga Nidra isn't empty; it's fertile, transformative, and profoundly healing.

Chakra meditation, another gem of the Indian tradition, focuses on the body's subtle energy centers. These chakras govern different aspects of our physical and emotional well-being, from safety and identity to love, intuition, and spiritual connection. When we meditate on these centers-using breath, color visualization, or affirmations, we invite balance and harmony into our system. As these energy centers open and align, we experience greater vitality, self-trust, and spiritual clarity. We begin to live from a more centered and integrated place, where intuition guides action and presence becomes power.

Sacred sound also plays a powerful role in meditation. Mantra and chanting meditation use vibrational repetition to still the mind and align us with higher consciousness. The ancient syllable Om, for example, is said to carry the frequency of creation itself. As we chant or silently repeat mantras, we're not just calming the mind, we're tuning ourselves like instruments, aligning with divine rhythm. Scientific research has shown that mantra meditation can enhance focus, reduce anxiety, and even shift brainwave patterns. But beyond science, it simply opens the heart, and connects us to something timeless and vast.

Beyond India, spiritual seekers have cultivated their own meditative languages. In the still monasteries of Japan, Zen meditation,or Zazen, teaches us the art of just sitting. With eyes half-open and attention inward, thoughts come and go like clouds in the sky. The practice isn't about seeking enlightenment; it's about realizing it's already here, in the stillness beneath all striving. Zen invites us to let go of effort, control, and the search itself, revealing a spacious presence that is always available when we stop trying to fix or change anything.

Then, from the poetic heart of the Middle East, comes Sufi meditation, a devotional, love-centered path that focuses on remembering the Divine. Through breathwork, music, or silent dhikr (remembrance), the practitioner surrenders the ego to the presence of the Beloved. The Sufi path isn't about discipline so much as it is about falling in love, with the divine, with the moment, with the soul. It softens us, expands our hearts, and draws us ever inward, where the mystic flame of longing reveals the unity behind all things.

Even in the modern world, mindfulness has emerged as a global bridge between ancient wisdom and contemporary life. Rooted in Buddhist teachings but embraced widely through secular frameworks, mindfulness is simply the practice of being fully present in each moment. It asks us to witness our thoughts, sensations, and emotions without judgment or attachment. In doing so, we reclaim our attention from distraction, and our power from autopilot. With time, mindfulness strengthens emotional resilience, clarity, and self-awareness, traits that not only improve our mental health but lead us toward living from a more authentic, integrated self.

Each of these practices, though diverse in form, points us in the same direction: inward. They are portals to the soul, guiding us home to our true nature. Whether you are drawn to the grounding rhythm of breath, the beauty of sacred sound, the silence of stillness, or the surrender of love, your path is valid. There is no hierarchy here, no perfect technique. Only what speaks to your soul.

Self-actualization is not a final destination, but an ever-deepening return, a peeling away of what is false so the real can rise. Through meditation, we learn not to become someone new, but to remember who we've always been. And in that remembrance, we awaken. One breath, one sacred moment at a time.

As you delve deeper into your spiritual journey and meditation practices, I invite you to explore something truly profound and heart-opening: Bhakti Yoga. Unlike the quiet contemplation of meditation or the analytical approach of self-inquiry, Bhakti is a path that speaks directly to the heart, inviting you to cultivate a deep, emotional connection with the Divine. It's the yoga of love, devotion, and surrender, where spiritual practice becomes an expression of your innermost feelings and reverence.

Bhakti Yoga doesn't require you to adhere to a particular belief system, it simply asks that you open your heart in service, chanting, prayer, or ritual. Whether it's singing devotional songs, repeating sacred mantras, or offering small acts of kindness, each act becomes a bridge that unites you with something greater. In this practice, devotion isn't a passive submission; it's an active, joyful surrender that transforms not only your relationship with the Divine but also your everyday life.

What makes Bhakti Yoga so special is that it takes the ordinary and makes it sacred. Every action becomes an offering, every moment an opportunity to deepen your connection to love and presence. So, if you're seeking a practice that infuses your spiritual life with tenderness and purpose, consider bringing Bhakti into your daily routine.

Let it fill your heart with devotion and watch how it transforms your world.

We live in a world that constantly pulls us towards accumulation, be it wealth, status, or possessions. but what if the pursuit of these things is not the key to happiness? What if, in fact, it's the attachment to them that keeps us tethered to a cycle of unfulfilled desires and endless striving?

Life, in its essence, is fleeting. From the moment we're born, we begin a journey towards an inevitable end. Yet, in our modern world, the pursuit of permanence and security often blinds us to the impermanence that surrounds us. The pursuit of material things can distract us from the deeper questions of life: What is my purpose? Why am I here? What truly matters? It is only when we embrace the transitory nature of life, when we let go of the illusion that we can control everything, that we can begin to live more authentically, more in tune with the flow of existence.

Alfred Ford, great-grandson of Henry Ford, is a remarkable example of someone who has integrated deep spirituality into a modern life of influence and responsibility. Embracing the path of Krishna Consciousness, he took spiritual initiation and became known as Ambarisha Dasa. Under the guidance of his guru, he committed himself to a life of devotion, service, and self-realization. His spirituality is not confined to personal practice, it also extends into his actions, philanthropy, and vision. As the driving force behind the Temple of the Vedic Planetarium in India, he demonstrates how spiritual conviction can inspire meaningful contributions to the world.

Steve Jobs, the visionary co-founder of Apple, experienced a profound spiritual transformation during his early years. Drawn to the teachings of Neem Karoli Baba, he traveled to

India in search of deeper meaning and insight. Although the saint had passed away shortly before his arrival, the influence of his philosophy, rooted in simplicity, self-awareness, and devotion, left a lasting impression on Jobs. He immersed himself in meditation and spiritual texts, particularly the book Autobiography of a Yogi, which he famously kept on his iPad and had distributed at his memorial service. For Jobs, spirituality became a foundation for clarity, intuition, and creative brilliance. His ability to think differently and design with purpose came not just from intellect, but from a quiet space of inner alignment that helped him rise above distraction and ego.

Mark Zuckerberg's spiritual exploration came through a more personal connection. Influenced by his visit to India with his wife, Priscilla, and encouraged by Steve Jobs, Zuckerberg journeyed to a temple dedicated to Neem Karoli Baba. Though his engagement with spirituality was quieter and more private, the experience marked a turning point in his search for purpose. He later spoke about how that visit helped him refocus during a challenging period in Facebook's early days. While not overtly religious, Zuckerberg's spiritual encounters offered him grounding and perspective, reinforcing the value of community, empathy, and meaningful connection, principles that increasingly shaped his personal and professional choices.

In the modern world of spiritual practice, few have explored the depths of this potential as thoroughly as Dr. Joe Dispenza. His work in Becoming Supernatural offers an eye-opening perspective on how meditation, combined with scientific understanding, can unlock the mind's hidden capabilities. One of the most intriguing concepts he explores is the role of the pineal gland, a small yet profoundly powerful organ within the brain that has long been associated with spiritual awakening and higher consciousness. For centuries, ancient traditions have revered the pineal gland as the "third eye", a portal to deeper states of awareness and connection to the divine. But Dispenza takes this ancient wisdom a step further, blending it with modern neuroscience to show us how we can activate this "third eye" to access a realm beyond the material world.

Through focused meditation, Dispenza teaches that we can tap into the pineal gland's power to produce neurochemicals like DMT, which is linked to altered states of consciousness, mystical experiences, and deep spiritual insights. By learning to activate this gland, we can transcend the limitations of ordinary perception and access higher states of awareness, where healing, transformation, and even supernatural experiences can occur.

What makes Dispenza's teachings so compelling is how he bridges science and spirituality. His approach demonstrates that meditation isn't just a tool for relaxation or stress reduction; it's a gateway to profound transformation. In activating the pineal gland, we align not only our body and mind but also our spirit, allowing us to break free from limiting thought patterns, past traumas, and material distractions. As we delve deeper into these practices, we begin to unlock a new reality, one that is rich with possibility, healing, and personal empowerment.

As you navigate your own path, I invite you to reflect on the impermanence of life. Meditation and spiritual practices are powerful tools that help you move beyond the distractions of the material world and reconnect with your true self. They offer you the opportunity to transcend the limitations of the ego, release attachments, and discover a deeper sense of purpose. Through surrender, service, and inner alignment, you can live a life of fulfillment that is not bound by external circumstances but is rooted in your spiritual connection to the greater whole.

Key notes from the chapter-

- Spirituality has always been part of us.
- No matter the culture or era, people have turned to spiritual practices to feel connected, grounded, and whole.
- Meditation is more than just quiet time.
- It helps us breathe easier, think clearer, and handle life with more calm and clarity.
- There's no one right way, just your way.
- Whether it's chanting, stillness, breathwork, or devotion, every path inward is valid if it speaks to your heart.
- Science backs what ancient wisdom knew.
- Studies show that mindfulness, prayer, and presence actually make us kinder, more resilient, and happier.
- We're capable of so much more.
- With practices like deep meditation, we can unlock higher awareness, heal deeply, and tap into our true potential.
- Real peace comes from within.
- The more we let go of chasing things outside of us, the more we find purpose, joy, and meaning inside.

Chapter 9:
From Zero to Hero

There is a quiet power in beginning from nothing, a kind of invisible force that shapes, chisels, and hardens an individual into something extraordinary. In modern culture, where the spotlight often blinds us to the backstage struggles behind every success story, it becomes easy to forget that greatness is rarely born from comfort. In a world obsessed with outcomes, where the media and people celebrate only the final glittering image of success, it is easy to forget that true greatness does not emerge fully formed. It is built quietly, stubbornly, in moments when giving up would have been easier, when no one was watching to offer praise, and yet the individual chose to endure. True excellence is not the child of ease. It is the child of adversity, persistence, and the fierce, private decision to keep going even when the road ahead seems endless. Greatness is not born under bright lights, but in the unseen, uncomfortable places where resilience is carved out of difficulty, one invisible choice at a time.

When life begins with little, when the path ahead is not already laid but must be carved step by step through effort and belief, something remarkable happens inside. Without the safety of ready-made support systems, the spirit is challenged to grow roots deeper than circumstance. Resilience is not something taught by words or inherited through comfort; it becomes a way of being, forged in the fires of necessity. The hunger for a better life, for safety, for meaning, for the dignity of standing on one's own two feet, awakens a fierce creativity and inner strength that might otherwise have remained dormant. With every obstacle faced and overcome, the individual uncovers a reservoir of courage, ingenuity, and endurance. Not because life made it easy, but precisely because it didn't. Each challenge becomes a silent mentor, each setback an invitation to dig deeper, adapt faster, and rise stronger. Over time, what began as lack transforms into a quiet, unshakable power, a self-made foundation no external force can easily erode.

Psychologist Abraham Maslow, in his famous theory known as the Hierarchy of Needs, described how human motivation works in layers, like a pyramid. At the very bottom of this pyramid are the most basic needs: food, water, shelter, and safety. Without these, nothing else matters. If a person is hungry or unsure where they'll sleep at night, they're not thinking about building a dream career, exploring creativity, or seeking inner peace. They're focused on staying alive.

When those basic needs are not met, something powerful happens in the mind. It goes into a kind of survival mode. Every decision, every thought becomes sharper, more focused. The mind is no longer drifting in comfort; it's alert, it's calculating, and it's trying to find a way out of discomfort. This heightened awareness isn't just stress, it's the brain's way of adapting to keep you going. In that state, people begin to develop skills they might never have tapped into otherwise. They become more resourceful, more observant, and far more determined.

Think about it like this: when you're backed into a corner, you're forced to become more creative. You start looking for solutions that aren't obvious. You notice small details that others miss. You learn to act quickly, to pivot when something doesn't work, and to endure discomfort without breaking down. This pressure, even though it feels heavy at times, trains the brain to keep moving forward no matter how unclear the path ahead might be.

Over time, this repeated exposure to uncertainty builds a kind of inner toughness. A person who has lived through hard times develops a mind that doesn't panic easily. They've already faced chaos. They've already learned how to navigate through fear, doubt, and scarcity. This doesn't just help them survive, it helps them succeed in ways that people who've never been tested might struggle to.

So while the lower levels of Maslow's hierarchy represent struggle, they are also where some of life's most important tools are forged. A strong sense of self, resilience, and the ability to keep going under pressure are not taught in textbooks. They are built in the real world, when you've had to figure out how to meet your needs with limited resources, and still find a way to hope for more.

Once a person feels safe and stable, Maslow explains that our motivation naturally shifts. We begin to seek connection, love, belonging, and meaningful relationships. Next comes the desire for esteem: to feel respected, capable, and valued. At the top of the pyramid is self-actualization, the deep fulfillment that comes from realizing one's full potential and living with purpose.

Maslow's hierarchy of needs

This phenomenon of resilience in the face of adversity is so intriguing that I had to bring up one of my absolute favourite books written by Nassim Nicholas Taleb, called Antifragile: Things That Gain from Disorder, the book argues that some systems actually benefit from shocks and volatility. Fragile things break under stress, but antifragile things grow stronger. Human beings who start life with adversity often embody this principle. Rather than collapsing under the weight of difficulties, they become tougher, smarter, and more capable precisely because of what they have endured. Taleb writes, "Wind extinguishes a candle and energizes fire." Those who face constant trials from an early stage are not snuffed out by the gales of misfortune; they are fanned into a fierce, enduring flame.

Empirical studies support this idea. Research in psychology has repeatedly shown that moderate levels of adversity can lead to higher levels of resilience and life satisfaction later on. A 2010 study published in the Journal of Personality and Social Psychology found that individuals who had experienced some lifetime adversity reported better mental health and greater ability to handle subsequent stress compared to those who had faced either high levels or no adversity at all. In other words, too little struggle can leave a person unprepared for life's inevitable hardships, while moderate struggle equips them with tools that make all the difference when true trials arrive.

This internal arsenal - resilience, emotional flexibility, self-reliance- cannot be bought or gifted. It must be forged through lived experience. When someone grows up needing to make every penny, every meal, every opportunity count, they develop a kind of grounded wisdom about life that no theoretical knowledge can substitute. They understand how to endure temporary defeats without letting go of the longer vision. They learn how to innovate when options are scarce, how to lead when no guidance is available, and how to believe in themselves even when no external validation exists.

Historical and contemporary examples echo this truth again and again. Oprah Winfrey's journey from rural poverty and childhood trauma to media mogul ship is not just a tale of success; it is a testimony to the transformative power of hardship. Howard Schultz, raised in a Brooklyn housing project, speaks often of how witnessing his father's struggle to find stable work fueled his drive to build Starbucks into a company where employees could feel respected and supported.

But perhaps more profound than the external accomplishments is the internal architecture that these struggles construct. Starting from scratch teaches patience , not the passive kind, but an active patience that knows how to persist intelligently, to refine strategies, to stay in the game when others surrender. It instills discipline, because shortcuts are rarely available when resources are scarce. It fosters a long-term vision, because immediate gratification is a luxury reserved for those who can afford it.

There is also a deeper gratitude that often accompanies those who rise from humble beginnings. When every achievement has been wrestled from the jaws of defeat, nothing is taken for granted. Success is not assumed, it is fought for and savored. Comfort is a blessing, not an expectation. This perspective creates a stability that is immune to the hollow anxieties that often plague those who have had too much, too soon. Where others crumble under the first signs of difficulty, those forged in hardship remember where they started, and they know they can build again, if necessary, from the ashes.

Of course, adversity alone is no guarantee of greatness. It is possible for hardship to embitter as much as it can strengthen. The critical difference lies in how the individual responds. Those who see adversity not as a personal curse but as a crucible for growth are the ones who transcend their beginnings. Viktor Frankl, the Holocaust survivor and author of Man's Search for Meaning, wrote that suffering ceases to be suffering the moment it finds meaning. Those who rise from nothing often find or create a meaning so strong that it propels them forward when all else would suggest surrender.

When viewed through this lens, humble beginnings are not a setback; they are a preparation. They are a schooling that teaches lessons too costly to be learned later in life. They are a tempering of the soul, a rigorous training of the mind and heart, a cultivation of a character that can bear the weight of real success.

To begin at zero is not to be cursed, but to be commissioned. It is a silent invitation to grow into someone who does not merely achieve but endures, not merely wins but transforms. Those who rise from nothing carry a strength that can neither be stolen nor undone. It is etched into their bones, woven into their spirit.

If you are at the beginning, if the climb ahead of you seems endless and steep, know this: you are in the company of giants. You are on the path where true greatness is born , not in the comfort of certainty, but in the fierce, relentless struggle of becoming.

The world may not recognize your roots. It may not see the nights you spent in silent battle, the mornings you dragged yourself up with hope scraped thin. But one day, when you stand tall, it will marvel at your strength. And you will know , deep in your bones , that it was not built in spite of your humble beginnings. It was built because of them.

When you look at someone like Arnold Schwarzenegger, it's easy to be amazed by what he achieved: world champion bodybuilder, Hollywood icon, Governor of California. But if you look a little closer, what's even more inspiring is where he started.

Arnold was born in 1947 in a small Austrian village, a world still scarred by the aftermath of war. His family had very little. The house he grew up in didn't have basic comforts, and luxuries were unheard of. Life wasn't easy, but it was simple: you worked hard, you respected discipline, and you didn't wait for anyone to hand you anything. That environment, harsh as it was, planted the early seeds of his character.

At fifteen, Arnold found bodybuilding, and it gave him a vision bigger than his village, bigger than anything he'd seen around him. Every single day, he trained. Not when he felt like it. Not when it was easy. Every day. He wasn't chasing fame at that point , he just knew he could be better, stronger, more. That simple commitment, repeated day after day, changed the course of his life.

When he came to America, he didn't blend in easily. His accent was thick, his name was unfamiliar, and his body didn't fit Hollywood's idea of a leading man. But he kept showing up. He worked on his speech, studied acting, took jobs that would put him closer to his dreams. Eventually, The Terminator happened , and the world knew his name. But long before the world knew, he had already decided who he was going to be.

Arnold's journey didn't stop with acting. He kept building , serving two terms as Governor of California, launching businesses, giving back through charity work, and encouraging young people to believe in their ability to change their lives. His book, Be Useful: Seven Tools for Life, captures the core lesson he lived by: don't wait for the world to recognize you. Become useful. Focus on doing the work. The recognition will come later. or maybe it won't. But the strength you build will stay with you either way.

Arnold's story reminds us that greatness isn't something you stumble into. It's built quietly, over time, in ordinary moments when no one is watching. It's built in the decision to practice when it's easier to quit. In choosing to believe in yourself when the odds say otherwise.

And that same power, the one that took a boy from a small village to the top of the world, is sitting inside you right now. You don't have to be born into opportunity. You don't need a perfect plan. You need a routine. You need patience. And you need the courage to take the next small step , even when you can't see the whole road ahead.

The truth is, you're never starting from nothing. You're starting from strength you haven't discovered yet.

You might be wondering, the data and the proven records are exemplary, but how could you start incorporating these values in your life? With these handy notes and compilation of ideas from some of the most brilliant minds, you could crack the code of zero to hero within no time.

- Reframe Your Story (Cognitive Behavioral Therapy Research)

When life gets heavy and difficulties hit without warning, most of us don't instantly rise to the occasion. Our first instinct is often quieter, more vulnerable, a wave of helplessness, a whisper of self-pity. We wonder why things seem so unfair. We wonder if something is wrong with us.

It's a natural response because, in those moments, the mind is simply trying to make sense of pain.

But there's a different way to meet those moments, a way that psychology, especially Cognitive Behavioral Therapy (CBT), has explored deeply. At the heart of it is one simple but powerful idea: how we interpret what happens to us shapes what happens next inside us.

Life will bring challenges; that part is inevitable. What changes everything is the story you tell yourself about those challenges. When you choose to ask, "What is this teaching me?" instead of sinking into defeat, something extraordinary happens in your brain. Research shows that this shift activates the regions responsible for problem-solving and creativity. You're not just coping anymore; you're evolving.

The beauty is that this isn't a one-time thing. Every time you reframe a tough experience , every time you look for meaning instead of simply absorbing the blow, you strengthen new pathways in your brain. Over time, your mind becomes more skilled at adapting. You build an internal toughness that isn't hard and brittle, but flexible, like the strongest kinds of steel.

It's important to understand: reframing doesn't erase pain. It doesn't sugarcoat real loss, heartbreak, or struggle. Pain deserves to be acknowledged, felt, and respected. But it doesn't have to define you. You are always bigger than what happens to you, and every difficulty, approached with the right mindset, can make that truth a little more real in your bones.

- Trust in Small Daily Efforts (Angela Duckworth's Grit Research)

One of the quiet misunderstandings about success is the belief that it comes from one big, life-changing moment, a breakthrough, a flash of genius, a lucky break. It's a comforting idea because it suggests that maybe success could just happen to us if we're lucky enough.

But when researchers like Angela Duckworth spent years studying the people who actually reached the highest levels , athletes, artists, entrepreneurs, leaders, a very different truth emerged. The most consistent trait among them wasn't talent. It wasn't intelligence. It was grit.

Grit isn't something flashy or loud. It's made up of small, steady choices, carried out quietly over a long period of time. It's showing up for practice when no one is watching. It's pushing through days when motivation feels a thousand miles away. It's holding onto a bigger vision even when the results feel painfully slow.

Imagine a tree deep underground, its roots weaving, strengthening, searching for water, long before anything ever breaks the surface. That's what grit looks like inside a person. Growth is happening, but it's not obvious yet. It's not glamorous. It doesn't get applause.

And that's exactly why it's so powerful.

The people who understand this, who trust the process of slow, patient effort, are the ones who eventually emerge looking like "overnight successes" to the outside world.

But there's really no such thing as an overnight success.

There are only people who worked for years in the dark, planting seeds, nurturing roots, quietly getting stronger, until one day, the world finally saw the fruits of what had been growing all along. As Matthew Syed explains in Bounce, Olympic-level success is not about innate talent but about focused, deliberate practice, often over 10,000 hours. It is grit, not gifts, that shapes greatness.

- Normalize Struggle (Carol Dweck's Growth Mindset Research)

When you're in the middle of a tough chapter, it can feel like you're uniquely cursed, like others must have had it easier.

But Carol Dweck's research on Growth Mindset shatters that illusion.

The people who achieve extraordinary things almost never glide through life without friction. In fact, what separates them isn't their lack of struggle, it's their relationship to struggle.

A fixed mindset believes, "If I'm struggling, I must not be good enough."

A growth mindset says, "If I'm struggling, it means I'm growing."

Dweck's studies show that those who normalize setbacks as a natural part of mastery persist far longer and ultimately succeed at higher levels.

Struggle is not a detour on the road to greatness; it is the road.

The sooner you stop seeing difficulty as a threat and start seeing it as an essential part of becoming who you are meant to be, the freer and more powerful you become.

- Build Your Psychological Immunity (Tal Ben-Shahar's Positive Psychology Research)

We all know about physical immunity, how vaccines expose us to small doses of viruses so we can fight off bigger infections later.

Tal Ben-Shahar, a pioneer in positive psychology, shows that the human mind has a similar system: psychological immunity.

Facing manageable levels of adversity, challenges that are hard but not overwhelming, strengthens our emotional resilience over time.

People who have lived completely sheltered lives often crumble at the first serious hardship.

Those who've weathered storms, learned to adapt, and rebuilt themselves after smaller failures develop mental toughness, the ability to stay grounded and hopeful even under pressure.

Adversity in moderate doses is not a trauma; it's a training ground.

Each challenge you survive adds another layer to your emotional armor, not making you colder or harder, but more flexible, wiser, and harder to defeat.

- Anchor Pain to Purpose (Viktor Frankl's Logotherapy Research)

If there's one human truth that stands above the rest, it's this: Pain is inevitable, but suffering is optional.

Viktor Frankl, A world-renowned psychiatrist and founder of logotherapy, discovered through personal experience and deep observation that those who survived were not necessarily the physically strongest, but those who could find meaning even in their suffering.

Frankl's Logotherapy teaches that human beings are meaning-makers. When life feels meaningless, even small hardships can feel unbearable. But when you tie your struggle to a purpose, when you see your pain as part of something larger than yourself, you unlock reserves of strength you didn't even know existed. Purpose transforms pain from something that cripples you into something that fuels you.

Whether your mission is to raise your children with love, create something lasting, serve your community, heal yourself, or live according to your deepest values, that mission gives your journey dignity, even when the road gets hard.

The above mentioned are just a couple curated studies and work from my liking, the ones that have stuck with me through times thick and thin, does nor mean you'd have to be compelled to resonate deeply with them, however, it always helps to have a sort of anchor, or a blueprint that you can keep going back to in times of doubt.

Success isn't about avoiding struggle or waiting for the stars to align in your favor. It's about what you do when the world doesn't hand you the perfect circumstances, how you choose to show up in the face of hardship, how you frame each setback as a learning opportunity, and how you persist when the road feels long and uncertain. What sets heroes apart from a nobody is not what they have at the moment, it is the way they act, think, and move, which is the greatest indicator of their character and outlook toward life, which ultimately propels them to self-actualization and success.

Key notes from the chapter-

1. Rock bottom is the starting point for transformation and not the end as most tend to believe-
2. Starting with nothing isn't a curse but a powerful foundation for growth. The journey to greatness often begins in moments of struggle, where the seeds of resilience and perseverance are planted.
3. Resilience and meaning are forged through suffering-
4. True strength comes from the ability to find purpose in adversity. Struggles are not setbacks, but lessons that build emotional toughness and mental clarity, shaping the individual into someone unshakable.
5. You can grow stronger from adversity if you adopt a growth mindset.
6. Embracing challenges as opportunities for growth rather than obstacles to avoid leads to lasting personal development. Those who view struggles as part of the process thrive where others falter.
7. Grit (passion + perseverance) matters more than talent for long-term success.
8. Success is built through consistent effort over time, not sudden breakthroughs. It's about showing up every day and staying focused on the long-term vision even when progress seems slow.
9. Small, aligned actions daily lead to massive change over time.
10. The key to success lies in the compounding power of daily habits, no matter how small. Each step forward, no matter how insignificant it seems at the time, is part of a larger journey towards self-actualization.

11. Your pain has a purpose-

Challenges are not signs of failure but stepping stones on the path to becoming your best self. Every painful experience adds depth to your character, shaping your resilience and ability to face future hardships with strength.

Chapter 10:
The Wealth Mindset: Aligning Inner Strength with Outer Success

When most people begin their journey toward financial independence, it starts with a job. A typical nine to five setup. A desk, a chair, a schedule. You show up every morning, work through the day, and collect a paycheck every month. For many, this feels like the responsible thing to do. And it is. In the beginning, you need that paycheck. It provides security. It keeps food on the table, rent paid, and helps you stand on your own feet. There is absolutely nothing wrong with starting here. It is where discipline is built. You learn to manage your time, communicate with others, operate within systems, and contribute to a larger mission. Your first job teaches you the basics of survival and professional growth. It introduces you to structure, expectations, deadlines, and the concept of trading your time for money. But that is also where the problem begins.

The moment you settle into that routine without a long term plan, you unknowingly fall into a trap. The trap is simple but dangerous. It is the idea that working harder, showing up every day, and following the rules will automatically lead to a better life. But the truth is, if you spend your whole life working for someone else, relying only on your salary, you will always be exchanging time for money. And time is not renewable. You can make back lost money. You cannot make back lost years. This model is inherently limiting. Even if you get promotions and raises, you are still stuck in a loop. You work for eight to ten hours a day, five or six days a week, and your income is always capped by your hours and energy. There is only so much of yourself you can give. And when your income depends entirely on your presence, freedom becomes impossible. You may be busy. You may even look successful. But real wealth, the kind that gives you peace and choice, stays out of reach.

The real goal is not just to earn more. It is to create a life where you no longer need to constantly trade your time to survive. Financial freedom is not about escaping work altogether. It is about choosing what kind of work you want to do, when, where, and for whom. It is about control over your time and energy. Imagine waking up in the morning not because your alarm goes off, but because you are excited about what you get to build or create. Imagine earning money not just from your job, but from the value you have created and the assets you own. That is true freedom. That is wealth. But this does not happen by accident. It happens when you become intentional. It happens when you shift your mindset from working to earn to working to build. From being a consumer to becoming a creator. From living paycheck to paycheck to investing in income streams that continue to grow without constant effort.

This is the exact shift Robert Kiyosaki speaks about in his book Rich Dad Poor Dad. It is not a how to guide to get rich quick, It is a philosophy. A change in how you think about money, education, and opportunity. Kiyosaki shares the story of his two father figures. One was highly educated, worked a secure government job, and believed in working hard for a paycheck. The other was an entrepreneur who understood money deeply and taught him about building wealth through ownership. The core message is that schools teach you to work for money, but not how money works. We are trained to become employees, not investors. To rely on income, not assets. This is where most people get stuck. They climb a ladder without realizing it is leaning against the wrong wall. Kiyosaki explains that the rich focus on buying or creating assets. An asset is anything that puts money in your pocket. A liability is anything that takes money out. This simple idea changes everything. A house you live in is not an asset if it drains your money. A car is not an asset just because it looks good. True assets generate cash flow. Think of rental properties, dividend-paying stocks, businesses, intellectual property, or even digital products. The goal is to build or acquire assets that work for you so that one day you do not have to.

Once you understand this, you begin to realize that the real game is not working harder but working smarter. It is about learning high-value skills, applying those skills to solve real problems, and eventually creating systems around those skills. In the beginning, you might still trade your time for money. You might consult, teach, build, or coach. But as you grow, the key is to shift from time-based income to value-based income. Instead of charging by the hour, you start charging for results. Eventually, you stop selling your time altogether and start creating value at scale. This is what separates a freelancer from a founder, or a worker from a creator. For example, someone with expertise in marketing can spend their entire career working for companies. Or they can eventually build a course, write a book, create content, or even start their own agency. The same skill. But used differently. One keeps you working forever. The other creates leverage.

This is the rich dad mentality. It is not about getting rich quick. It is about becoming financially intelligent. It is about thinking like an owner, even while you are still an employee. It is about using your job to fund your future, not just your present. Every paycheck is an opportunity to invest. In stocks. In knowledge. In a side hustle. In your own business.

In yourself. You can start small. You can build quietly. But you must begin. Because no one is coming to rescue you. Not your employer. Not the government. Not the system. Your freedom is your responsibility. And it begins with awareness.

I would like to talk about a personal anecdote, which is in line with the teachings above. In my first two years of corporate life in the UK, I overlooked pension contributions, assuming they were irrelevant at that stage. It was a costly oversight. Once I understood the long-term benefits, I began contributing and discovered that every contribution I made was matched by my employer, effectively doubling my investment. With private pensions, the government adds tax relief, meaning even more money goes into your pot. Over time, this compounds into a substantial fund for retirement. Similarly, I began investing in mutual funds like the S&P 500 and NSE 150, which historically offer average annual returns between 8 to 12 percent. These broad index funds are diversified, low-cost, and ideal for long-term wealth creation. The key insight was this: consistent investing, even in small amounts, backed by time and compound growth, can quietly build real financial independence. However I am not an investment advisor and you need to speak to your financial advisor and my case is just an example and not an investment advice.

There is a modern thinker who embodies this awareness better than almost anyone today. His name is Naval Ravikant. An entrepreneur and angel investor, Naval is known not only for his success in Silicon Valley but for his clarity of thought. He co-founded AngelList and invested early in companies like Twitter and Uber. But what sets him apart is not just his financial success. It is the wisdom he shares so openly about wealth, happiness, and personal growth. His ideas have been compiled in a book called The

Almanack of Naval Ravikant, curated by Eric Jorgenson, which is available for free online. It is one of the most powerful guides to modern wealth creation. Naval's philosophy is rooted in freedom. He does not just talk about money. He talks about how to design a life of meaning and peace. His approach to wealth is simple yet profound. He believes that wealth is about owning assets that earn while you sleep. Money is just a tool. Status is a game. But wealth is freedom.

Naval speaks often about the importance of leverage. In the past, leverage came from labor. You hired people to work for you. Today, leverage comes from capital, code, and content. If you can write code, you can build products that scale infinitely. If you can write or speak, you can reach millions through content. If you can manage capital, you can invest in businesses that grow without your presence. Naval emphasizes the value of specific knowledge. This is knowledge that is unique to you. It cannot be easily taught or copied. It often looks like play to you but work to others. The internet allows you to scale this specific knowledge in ways that were not possible before. He advises you to productize yourself. To take what you are good at and package it in a way that can reach thousands or even millions. This could be a newsletter, a podcast, a YouTube channel, an online course, a book, a startup, anything that multiplies your effort through technology. He also reminds us to play long-term games with long-term people. Trust compounds just like money. Reputation is the ultimate currency. If you act with integrity, stay patient, and focus on creating value, the returns will come. He rejects the toxic hustle culture and instead promotes clarity, creativity, and calmness. As he says, escape competition through authenticity. No one can beat you at being you.

The beauty of Naval's ideas is that they are timeless and practical. They apply whether you are just starting out or already deep in your career. They encourage you to look beyond the short-term hustle and start building real wealth. Not just financial wealth but inner wealth. The kind of wealth that gives you time, peace, health, and purpose. By integrating the mindset of Rich Dad and the wisdom of Naval Ravikant, you can design a life that is not just productive but truly fulfilling. You start where you are. You use your job as a launchpad. You build skills, invest wisely, and gradually create assets. You focus on learning, leverage, and long-term thinking. Over time, you shift from surviving to thriving.

Up until now, we've focused on the outer game, specifically on building wealth through leverage, learning, and long-term thinking. We have looked at how you can use capital, code, content, and specific knowledge to create financial freedom and design a life on your own terms, which is, quite important. Material wealth gives you options, It buys back your time, creates safety, and opens doors that once felt closed. But if we stop there, we miss the deeper point. Because what good is financial freedom if you feel empty inside? What's the value of success if you're constantly anxious, burnt out, or chasing validation? The truth is, no amount of money can substitute for inner peace and no amount of achievement can fill the space where purpose and self-worth are meant to live.

That's why the journey doesn't end with external success, it deepens into something richer. Real abundance is holistic. It isn't just about how much you have, but how you feel, how you live, and who you become in the process. Inner wealth is the soil from which all sustainable outer success grows. Without it, your wins will feel hollow. With it, even your small steps will feel deeply satisfying. So, shifting our focus inward, Let's explore the wealth that can't be counted but can be felt in every moment of clarity, calm, connection, and truth. Because that is where true prosperity begins, not quite in the numbers, but in the nourishment of your soul.

In a world that celebrates visible achievements, material wealth, and external validation, the idea of inner wealth often gets overlooked or misunderstood. People chase after success, status, and money as if these things alone can guarantee happiness or fulfillment. But beneath all the noise and glitter, there lies a truth that every spiritually awakened person eventually realizes. Real, lasting abundance begins within. Inner wealth is not a vague or mystical idea. It is a deep reservoir of emotional balance, spiritual alignment, mental clarity, self-worth, and inner peace. It is the invisible foundation upon which all meaningful and sustainable success is built. Without it, even the most glamorous life can feel hollow. With it, even the simplest life can feel complete.

This inner strength allows you to experience the present moment fully, to live with purpose rather than pressure, and to navigate adversity without losing yourself. It gives you access to your inner resources such as resilience, intuition, compassion, courage, and faith that help you deal with life's inevitable ups and downs. It allows you to live from a place of grounded confidence rather than anxiety or comparison. In today's fast-moving, success-obsessed world, this internal richness becomes your compass, your anchor, and your sanctuary. The irony is that when people lack this internal richness, they often try to fill the void with more money, more stuff, more achievements, or more praise. But no amount of external gain can substitute for a lack of self-worth, peace, or connection.

What makes this inner foundation so powerful is that it directly impacts your ability to manifest outer wealth.

When you are internally abundant, meaning you live in gratitude, self-belief, and energetic alignment, you naturally attract opportunities, people, and experiences that match that frequency. The law of attraction is not just a spiritual principle but also has psychological and neurological roots. When you believe in your worth and see yourself as enough, you act in ways that reflect confidence and clarity. Your decisions are not fear-based or reactive. You do not settle or sabotage. You stay open to possibilities. Neuroscience supports this. Practices that foster self-trust like gratitude, mindfulness, and visualization actually rewire the brain. Studies show that gratitude activates the brain's reward system and increases dopamine, which enhances focus, motivation, and overall happiness. Meditation strengthens the prefrontal cortex, the part of the brain responsible for decision-making and awareness. These internal changes create the conditions necessary for external success. You stop hustling from a place of lack and start creating from a place of wholeness.

Manifestation is about alignment. And alignment begins with emotional clarity and spiritual congruence. When you are clear about who you are and what you value, you begin to make choices that support your highest good. You are not swayed by distractions or driven by desperation. You invest in growth, you show up with integrity, and you set boundaries that protect your energy. These behaviors create momentum. They invite in more of what you want, whether it is financial abundance, creative opportunities, deep relationships, or physical well-being. Fulfillment fuels manifestation because it creates coherence between what you desire and how you live. If you are chasing abundance but feel like you are not enough, you are sending mixed signals to both your subconscious and the universe. But if you embody abundance, even before the outer proof arrives, you magnetize it faster. This practice teaches you to embody the future version of yourself now, not someday when things are perfect, but today, from within.

There is also a practical link between a healthy mindset and material success. People who cultivate emotional and mental well-being manage their money with more awareness. They are less likely to make impulsive purchases for validation and more likely to spend and invest in alignment with their values. They are generous, but not self-sacrificing. They give from overflow, not obligation. They understand that money is energy, and how they relate to it reflects how they relate to themselves. If you feel unworthy internally, you will unconsciously repel or misuse financial abundance. But if you feel safe, whole, and deserving, you will attract and sustain it with ease.

Research from Harvard and Stanford shows that people who operate from a sense of purpose and internal clarity tend to perform better, lead more effectively, and recover faster from setbacks. These qualities translate directly into professional and financial success. The strength of your internal life shows up in how you handle pressure, how you communicate, how you lead, how you love, and how you receive. It shows up in your capacity to say no when something is not aligned and to say yes to your calling without needing external permission.

Cultivating this foundation is a practice, a process, and a commitment. It means choosing gratitude when it is easier to complain. It means listening to your intuition even when logic argues otherwise. It means trusting in divine timing instead of forcing outcomes. It means learning from failure instead of being defined by it. And perhaps most of all, it means valuing who you are over what you achieve. That is the paradox. The moment you no longer need the external to validate your worth, it begins to flow to you more effortlessly. Not because you are chasing it, but because you are aligned with it.

Sustainable wealth is holistic. It includes your emotional well-being, physical vitality, mental clarity, spiritual peace, and financial stability. To cultivate wealth in all these aspects, it helps to start small and consistently nurture healthy habits. Physically, this may mean investing in your health through nutrition, exercise, and rest. Emotionally, it may require therapy, journaling, or intentional connection with supportive people. Mentally, it involves lifelong learning and cognitive discipline. Spiritually, it means practices that align you with higher purpose. Financially, it means learning how money works, how to save, how to invest, and how to create value. The more aligned these aspects are, the more stable and joyful your external life becomes.

Real-life financial wealth follows principles that mirror inner abundance. You must have a vision. You must take consistent action. You must delay gratification. You must manage risk. You must invest in what matters long term. These are the same principles that apply to building self-worth and inner clarity. Just as compound interest works in financial investments, daily deposits of self-care and awareness yield exponential returns in confidence and peace. A person who practices discipline, intentional living, and vision both inside and outside is more likely to create sustainable success.

In today's world, it is easy to fall into the trap of defining success only by what can be measured. Social media amplifies this by putting a spotlight on material accomplishments. The size of your house, the brand of your clothes, the destinations you travel to all become signals of worth. Yet the research tells another story. A study published in Nature Human Behaviour in 2021 showed that beyond a certain income level, additional earnings do not significantly increase day-to-day happiness. The emotional return on financial investment plateaus. What continues to increase well-being is a sense of purpose, deep relationships, and emotional stability.

Dr Martin Seligman, a pioneer in positive psychology, introduced the PERMA model which identifies five pillars of well-being: positive emotion, engagement, relationships, meaning, and achievement. Material wealth can support these areas, but it cannot replace them. A million-dollar bank account does not guarantee a meaningful life. But a life rooted in connection, authenticity, and service can feel wealthy regardless of the numbers. This is why spiritual depth and emotional clarity are inseparable from long-term success. When you live with spiritual intention, your actions align with your soul. You are not chasing success for approval or identity. You are creating it as an extension of your truth.

Spiritual practices such as meditation, gratitude journaling, breathwork, or prayer are not just feel-good habits. They are tools that ground you, clear your mind, and reconnect you to your higher self. Science backs this up. A meta-analysis published in JAMA Internal Medicine in 2014 concluded that mindfulness meditation significantly reduces symptoms of anxiety and depression. Meditation also increases gray matter in parts of the brain associated with learning, memory, and emotional regulation. This means that your inner practices literally reshape your mind and body in ways that support long-term success.

Every decision you make either builds or drains your inner clarity and inner peace. Saying yes to your values, prioritizing rest, cultivating joy, and practicing forgiveness are all deposits in your internal bank. Ignoring your intuition, living in comparison, and chasing approval are withdrawals. The more aware you become of these dynamics, the more intentional you can be in how you live. You are not here just to survive or perform. You are here to thrive and contribute from a place of fullness.

The truth is that building this foundation is the gateway to everything you desire. It is not a luxury or an afterthought. It is the beginning. Whether your dream is to write a book, build a business, raise a family, or travel the world, it will be more joyful and successful if it is rooted in self-worth, clarity, and peace. And that is what cultivating internal richness gives you. It is the most important investment you will ever make. Because from it, all other riches grow.

Key notes from the chapter-

- Start with earning, grow into building.
- A job teaches discipline, but true wealth begins when you shift from trading time for money to creating value and assets that grow over time.
- Work smarter, not just harder.
- Wealth comes from leverage- using tools like capital, code, and content to scale your skills and income beyond your daily hours.
- Invest early and consistently.
- Small, steady contributions, whether to pensions or mutual funds, compound over time and can quietly build real financial independence.
- Mindset shapes your money life.
- When you think like an owner, not just a worker, you begin to invest in skills, assets, and decisions that serve your long-term freedom.

- Inner peace fuels outer success.
- Financial freedom means nothing if you're burned out or empty inside. Emotional balance, purpose, and clarity are your real wealth.
- True abundance is aligned living.
- When your actions, values, and energy are in sync, success flows naturally, not just in your bank account, but in how you feel every day.

Chapter 11:

The Essence of Time: Staying Ahead in a Fast-Paced World

Timing quietly governs the direction of progress. While it often escapes attention, it is one of the most decisive elements shaping outcomes today. In a world where information spreads within seconds and technologies evolve overnight, the ability to recognize and respond to the right moment can open doors that hard work alone cannot. There is a silent intelligence to time that rewards presence, awareness, and aligned action.

Everything around us reflects the truth that time carries energy. Seeds turn to trees when nurtured in the right season. Tides rise and fall without force. The human body follows cycles of wakefulness and rest. Within these natural patterns is a kind of wisdom that invites us to pause and notice when the conditions are ready, when to begin, when to act with confidence, and when to simply wait without resisting.

Artificial intelligence has added a new tempo to this era. What once required months of research, planning, and production can now be condensed into days or even hours. Ideas can be tested in real time, content can be created in moments, and decisions can be supported by a wealth of data that was previously inaccessible. This shift brings both opportunity and urgency. In this new rhythm, those who are able to sense the right moment and act with clarity are the ones who often move ahead. The pace of change invites quick adaptation and focused execution, not because speed is a race, but because opportunities now have shorter windows before they shift again.

Timing does not speak loudly. It shows itself through intuition, patterns, subtle signals, and quiet internal cues. There may be a moment where everything feels open, where hesitation fades, and direction becomes clear. Acting from that place allows effort to flow without resistance. There is no need for excessive push, because things begin to align on their own. There is a kind of ease that shows up when decisions are made at the right time.

In the modern world, decisions are no longer solely based on effort or logic. They are also shaped by how tuned in someone is to the environment around them. The evolution of technology, the rise of new markets, and the shifting behavior of consumers all reflect the speed at which circumstances are evolving. When someone pays close attention to these signals, they are better equipped to act in alignment with what is unfolding. That alignment leads to impact that feels effortless, not because it is easy, but because it is timely.

There is an example often observed in creative fields and innovation circles. A product or idea might be introduced at the exact moment when people are searching for it, even if they did not realize it yet. The timing alone elevates the reception. The same idea shared earlier or later might not receive the same response. This does not reduce the value of the idea itself, but it shows how timing enhances relevance. When something meets a moment of need or desire, it resonates more deeply. That resonance leads to trust, growth, and lasting connection.

Timing also applies to the individual level. Every person has their own internal rhythm. There are moments in the day when energy feels high, clarity is sharper, and creativity feels natural. Honoring those windows can improve focus and performance without the need for longer hours or more effort. These cycles are unique to each person, and learning how to work with them allows for deeper engagement with tasks that matter most. Productivity becomes less about constantly being busy and more about choosing when to do meaningful work with intention.

When it comes to big decisions, timing can shift outcomes in powerful ways. There are moments when all signs point toward movement. The body feels steady, the mind feels ready, and the environment offers a sense of support. Taking action in those moments leads to breakthroughs. There is no need for the moment to be dramatic. Sometimes it arrives quietly. The mind may have questions, but the deeper part of the self feels certain. Trusting that feeling can shape the course of a journey.

In the same way, there are also times to observe, listen, and wait. Waiting does not always mean inaction. It can be a conscious choice to gather clarity, to allow new insights to arrive, or to sense what is unfolding before stepping in. Stillness has its own intelligence. It is during these moments that new paths often reveal themselves, not through force, but through presence. Being fully in the moment allows timing to become a guide rather than an obstacle.

Technology will continue to evolve. Artificial intelligence will become more integrated into daily life. Markets will expand and collapse. Tools will change. But through all of this, one principle will remain steady. Those who are attuned to time will continue to move with grace through uncertainty. They will not be overwhelmed by the speed of change because they are not reacting to it. They are listening to it. They are responding to it with awareness and thoughtful precision.

The beauty of timing lies in its neutrality. It favors no one and excludes no one. It is available to those who choose to notice it. Developing a relationship with time is not about gaining control over it. It is about creating harmony with it. When there is harmony with time, there is no struggle to be everywhere at once. There is clarity on where to be and when to move.

To practice this way of living, begin with observation. Notice the hours when you feel most focused. Notice the tasks that feel easier at certain times. Pay attention to your environment. Watch how situations evolve. Learn how long it takes for an idea to take root and grow. Give yourself permission to pause and listen before you act. These are not delays, These are acts of alignment.

Opportunities come in waves. When they are met with readiness, transformation happens quickly. That readiness does not come from constant motion. It comes from presence. Knowing what is needed, what is unfolding, and how your action fits into the broader movement of events. This creates momentum that is sustainable. It builds from clarity, not urgency.

In a world that is constantly in motion, it is easy to mistake urgency for importance. But when timing is understood and honored, there is no need to rush. Action becomes intentional. Work becomes aligned. Results arrive with more depth and less friction. The path becomes clearer, not because it is free of challenges, but because the choices are guided by a deeper sense of right timing.

As the world continues to evolve, those who thrive will be those who remain present. They will not need to predict every change. They will simply be in tune with the current moment. They will know when to move, when to wait, and when to adjust. This sense of timing will support their growth, their creativity, and their resilience.

When time becomes a partner, life begins to open in ways that feel effortless and fulfilling. The power of when is already available. It lives in silence, in awareness, in stillness, and in motion. And when it is honored, it brings with it the quiet confidence that everything is unfolding exactly as it should.

Time influences everything, from the choices we make in a single day to the trajectory of our lives. We often focus on the goals we want to achieve or the habits we wish to cultivate, but rarely do we pay attention to when we are most likely to succeed. This oversight has major consequences, especially when it comes to procrastination. If left unchecked, procrastination is not just a harmless delay tactic. It quietly chips away at our potential, self-worth, and overall well-being.

Procrastination is the silent killer of progress.Procrastination is the greatest enemy of time, it steals our most valuable resource by turning minutes into hours of delay and indecision. In today's fast-paced world, where success is often determined by how swiftly and efficiently we act, procrastination becomes a silent saboteur, hindering growth, disrupting momentum, and keeping us stuck while the world moves forward without pause. It hides behind every moment we say "I'll do it tomorrow," every incomplete project, and every resolution we postpone. It convinces us that we are simply waiting for the right moment, but that moment rarely arrives. According to a longitudinal study published in BMC Psychology, procrastination is a strong predictor of depressive symptoms and increased stress levels, particularly in students over time. What feels like a temporary relief actually becomes a long-term burden.

People procrastinate for various reasons. It could be fear of failure, perfectionism, a lack of structure, or simply an overwhelmed mind. Interestingly, procrastination has little to do with laziness. Procrastination isn't a sign of laziness. Most people who procrastinate are smart and capable. It just so happens that they struggle to manage difficult emotions. When a task feels boring, stressful, or uncertain, the brain looks for a quick escape, like scrolling on your phone or doing something easier. This brings short-term relief, but it leads to long-term stress, guilt, and self-doubt.

In today's fast-paced world, where everything moves quickly and we're constantly distracted, it's even harder to stay focused. The pressure to keep up makes us more likely to avoid uncomfortable tasks. But procrastination doesn't just delay work, it can hurt our health, career, relationships, and confidence. It eats away time, a valuable asset in a fast paced generation

Every time we put something off, we send ourselves the message that we can't be trusted to take action. Over time, that belief sticks. The good news is, procrastination is not a permanent flaw, it's a habit tied to how we handle emotions. Once we understand that, we can learn better ways to respond, manage time, fulfill tasks efficiently, take control, and rebuild trust in ourselves.

But there is hope. And that hope begins with self-awareness and intentional change. Understanding our procrastination habits is the first step toward reversing them. When we shine a light on the behavior without judgment, we can begin to dismantle its power over us. We can then turn to evidence-based strategies that have helped many others break the cycle.

One practical method is the Two Minute Rule. This approach is simple. If a task takes less than two minutes to complete, do it immediately. Send that quick email. Wash that coffee mug. Make that phone call. Often, the hardest part is starting. By making the entry point as easy and quick as possible, we bypass the brain's natural resistance. This method works because it creates momentum. Once we get started, we are more likely to continue.

Another highly effective tool is creating implementation intentions. This technique, supported by psychological research, involves forming a clear plan that connects a specific situation with a desired behavior. For example, saying, "At 7 p.m. I will begin my presentation outline," is far more powerful than vaguely saying, "I'll work on the presentation tonight." The brain responds well to specificity and structure. People who use implementation intentions are significantly more likely to achieve their goals.

Time blocking is another strategy that can drastically reduce procrastination. By setting aside specific chunks of time for particular tasks, we remove the open-ended nature of to-do lists and give our responsibilities a defined space in our schedule. This reduces decision fatigue, enhances focus, and creates accountability. Even if distractions arise, you are more likely to return to your plan when your day has a built-in rhythm.

But to truly master productivity and reduce procrastination, we must look beyond structure. We must also look inward; specifically at our natural biological rhythms. Dr. Michael Breus, in his book "The Power of When," introduces the concept of chronotypes. A chronotype is your internal biological clock, and it affects when you feel most alert, creative, focused, and tired. Breus categorizes people into four main chronotypes: Lions, Bears, Wolves, and Dolphins.

Lions are early risers and feel most productive in the morning. Bears follow the solar cycle and perform best during traditional work hours. Wolves are night-oriented and thrive later in the day. Dolphins are light sleepers with irregular energy patterns and often feel their best mid-morning. Knowing your chronotype allows you to align your tasks with your natural peaks of energy and focus.

For instance, if you are a Lion, it makes sense to schedule your most demanding or creative tasks in the early morning. If you are a Wolf, those same tasks may be better tackled in the evening. Understanding your body's natural cues helps you schedule work during times when it feels less like a fight. This reduces resistance and makes procrastination less tempting.

When you begin scheduling your life based on your internal clock, you notice something remarkable. Tasks begin to flow. Creativity increases. Focus sharpens. You no longer rely on willpower alone. Instead, you build systems that work with you, not against you. This does not mean life becomes perfect or that motivation is always high, but it becomes easier to stay on track because the structure now supports your natural tendencies.

Another important aspect of beating procrastination is learning to appreciate small wins. Neuroscience shows that each time we complete a task, our brain releases a small dose of dopamine. This reward mechanism boosts motivation and encourages us to keep going. By breaking tasks into smaller, manageable parts and completing them step by step, we can create a loop of positive reinforcement. Over time, this builds momentum and replaces the habit of avoidance with one of consistent action.

Finally, self-compassion is essential in the journey to overcoming procrastination. We all fall behind sometimes.

We all delay. But what separates progress from paralysis is how we respond when we fall short. Harsh self-criticism only deepens the cycle. Self-compassion, on the other hand, offers us the grace to acknowledge the delay, learn from it, and return to our goals with renewed intention.

Time is not just a calendar or a clock. It is a personal rhythm, an emotional space, and a tool that, when used wisely, can change everything. By recognizing when we work best, honoring our energy patterns, and applying proven psychological strategies, we can shift from procrastination to purpose. The power of when is not about squeezing more into your day. It is about aligning your efforts with your nature. It is about finding the sweet spot where action feels natural and results become inevitable.

Time is the ultimate currency in our rapidly evolving world. No one demonstrates this truth better than Elon Musk, whose bold ventures like Tesla, SpaceX, the Boring Company, and now Optimus, the humanoid robot, illustrate how speed, vision, and fearless innovation can transform entire industries and even the future itself. Musk's journey reveals that success today requires more than good ideas; it demands swift action and the ability to execute those ideas at an unprecedented pace.

Tesla is perhaps the clearest example of how moving fast can disrupt established systems. The company did not wait for the electric car to become mainstream or for decades of research to unfold before releasing its groundbreaking vehicles. Instead, it pressed forward aggressively, developing electric cars that challenged the very notion of what an automobile could be. Tesla's rapid advancement in battery technology, vehicle design, and software updates allowed it to outpace industry giants that were slow to adapt. Over the air software updates alone changed how cars are maintained and improved after purchase, something traditional manufacturers did not anticipate. This relentless drive created not just a product, but a new vision for transportation and sustainability.

SpaceX's story is equally remarkable. Musk dared to take on the immense challenge of space travel with the goal of reducing costs and increasing access to the final frontier. By designing rockets that could be reused multiple times, SpaceX broke decades of aerospace tradition. What once was a costly, one-time use process became a rapidly repeatable, cost-efficient operation. This breakthrough was not the result of slow trial and error but of intense focus, rapid iteration, and a willingness to learn from failure quickly. SpaceX changed the game for space exploration, inspiring an entire industry to rethink what was possible.

The Boring Company adds another layer to this narrative. Faced with the persistent problem of traffic congestion, Musk envisioned a network of tunnels beneath cities to ease surface traffic. Rather than waiting for governments or large urban planners to solve this problem in their own time, he took swift action, rapidly prototyping tunnel designs and beginning construction projects. This company highlights the idea that innovation is not just about high tech gadgets or space travel. It can also be about practical solutions that improve daily life, and the key to success is acting quickly before challenges become overwhelming.

Optimus, the humanoid robot, embodies the future of rapid innovation. As artificial intelligence and robotics evolve at breakneck speed, Musk's vision is to create robots that handle repetitive or dangerous tasks such as defence purposes, allowing humans to focus on creativity and problem solving. The pace of development in this space means that what once belonged only in science fiction is now being built and tested in real time. This reflects a larger truth: in the age of AI, waiting to catch up is not an option.

Leaders and innovators must leap forward, embracing new tools to accelerate progress and redefine what is possible.

What unites these ventures is a deep understanding of the value of time. In this new era, time is no longer a background factor; it is the driving force behind competitiveness and success. The ability to adopt and implement new technologies quickly separates those who lead from those who follow. Waiting for perfect conditions or ideal circumstances means falling behind. Bold, rapid moves are required to capitalize on the shifting landscape.

This urgency is not merely about speed for speed's sake. It is about creating momentum and resilience in a world where technological advances happen daily. The traditional timeline for innovation has compressed from years to months, or even weeks. The AI revolution intensifies this pace, offering tools that amplify human capabilities and open new possibilities overnight. Harnessing this momentum means thinking differently about how and when to act.

Companies that cling to old ways of working find themselves outpaced by agile competitors who build, test, and iterate faster. Similarly, individuals who delay adapting their skills or embracing new technologies risk missing out on opportunities. Speed combined with a clear vision becomes a powerful formula for sustained success.

Elon Musk's approach also shows that speed must be balanced with a willingness to take risks and learn from failure. The culture at his companies encourages experimentation and accepts setbacks as part of progress. This mindset prevents stagnation and fosters innovation that can quickly respond to new information or challenges. Being fast does not mean rushing blindly but moving decisively and adjusting course as needed.

For anyone seeking to thrive in this era, the message is clear. The age of AI demands that you act now. Waiting for the right moment often leads to missed chances. Instead, develop a habit of rapid learning, embrace new tools, and take deliberate steps toward your goals. Each small, timely action builds momentum that compounds over time. The faster you adapt, the more leverage you gain.

Ultimately, the power of when is about aligning your efforts with the speed of change. It is about moving in rhythm with the new realities of technology and market dynamics. Speed unlocks opportunities and builds confidence, turning uncertainty into progress. Elon Musk's journey teaches us that vision paired with rapid execution reshapes what is possible.

In this world, time is not just a measurement; it is the most valuable resource we have. Those who master the power of when, who move with urgency and clarity, will shape the future instead of watching it unfold from the sidelines.

Time is the foundation upon which all success is built. It is the thread that weaves potential into reality. Understanding the importance of time and learning how to leverage it effectively is essential for unlocking your ultimate potential. When you recognize that each moment is an opportunity to move closer to your goals, you begin to harness a power greater than talent or resources alone.

The ability to act swiftly, to pivot when necessary, and to continuously learn accelerates growth in ways that mere planning cannot. Every decision you make to embrace the moment, to seize the present, and to engage fully with the now compounds over time, creating a momentum that propels you forward.

Leaders like Elon Musk illustrate that it is not enough to dream big. You must also move fast to turn those dreams into reality. In a world reshaped by technology and artificial intelligence, time itself becomes the measure of your success. The faster you align yourself with the current of change, the greater your impact will be.

Ultimately, mastering the power of when means living with intention and urgency. It means recognizing that time waits for no one and that your future depends on the actions you take today. By leveraging time wisely, you unlock doors to opportunities, growth, and fulfillment that would otherwise remain closed. Time is not just what you have—it is who you become.

Key notes from the chapter-

- Time is energy,move in rhythm, not in rush.
- Like nature's cycles, success flows when you act with alignment, not pressure. The right moment often whispers, not shouts.
- Procrastination steals your potential.
- It's not laziness, but emotion-driven delay. By understanding and managing your internal resistance, you reclaim your time and power.
- Use your body clock as a compass.
- Your chronotype-Lion, Bear, Wolf, or Dolphin, affects focus and creativity. Align tasks with your natural energy peaks to reduce friction and boost results.
- Small starts create big momentum.
- Tools like the Two-Minute Rule, time blocking, and celebrating small wins help you bypass resistance and build sustainable action habits.
- Speed meets success when paired with clarity.

- Elon Musk's ventures show that rapid execution, learning from failure, and embracing AI create unmatched innovation and impact.
- Time is your greatest leverage.
- When you act with intention and urgency, you multiply your growth. The future belongs to those who don't just plan- but move.

Chapter 12:

Think Big, Move Fast: Mastering Ideation to Execution

There's a familiar moment that arrives in all of our lives, a lightning bolt of insight that seems to split open the sky of our routine thinking. It might strike in the middle of a workout, during a long commute, or just before sleep begins to cradle the mind. The idea arrives with force and clarity, a business that solves a real need, a book that tells a powerful story, a social cause that stirs your heart, or a tool that would make lives easier. It feels revolutionary, like you've just stumbled upon a key the world has been waiting for.

But what happens next? More often than not, nothing.

The idea is written down in a notebook that gets shelved, or entered into a note-taking app never to be opened again. Days turn into weeks, weeks into months, and the idea dies a quiet death in the graveyard of intentions. One day, you see someone else doing something strikingly similar, launching a product, publishing a book, building a movement. That jolt of envy and regret hits you in the gut. You tell yourself, I had that idea first. And you probably did. But they executed. You didn't.

This pattern is more common than we care to admit. We've glorified inspiration and fantasized about eureka moments, yet the truth is much more grounded. Ideas are abundant. It's execution that's rare and precious.

According to a study by Harvard Business Review, over 70 percent of strategies fail due to poor execution, not poor ideation. Ideas alone are not what shape our lives. It is the capacity to act on them, consistently and courageously, that determines who succeeds and who stays stuck in a cycle of what-ifs.

Think of the world's most influential entrepreneurs, authors, athletes, or inventors. While each had a vision, it was their relentless commitment to bring that vision into reality through setbacks, rejection, boredom, and fear that separated them from the millions who had similar ideas but no momentum. Execution is the bridge between imagination and impact.

Why, then, do so many fail to cross that bridge?

The answer lies in how we live our days. Success is not created in sporadic bursts of brilliance. It's cultivated in habits. Our habits shape our mindset, direct our focus, and determine whether we consistently move forward or simply dream in circles. As James Clear masterfully put it in Atomic Habits, "You do not rise to the level of your goals, You fall to the level of your systems."

This means that the greatest ideas will remain locked in your mind unless you design daily behaviors that support their manifestation.

Let's say you have an idea for a podcast. You're passionate, you've identified a niche, and you know people would benefit from your message. That's ideation, But execution? That's the daily process of writing outlines, scheduling interviews, learning editing software, promoting each episode even when no one's listening yet. It's setting aside the time, protecting your focus, and pushing through awkwardness, learning curves, and zero likes. It's about being willing to be bad before you get good.

But execution doesn't just require action. It requires managing the inner world, self-doubt, perfectionism, fear of judgment. One of the biggest myths about execution is that you'll feel ready. You won't. Readiness is not a feeling. It's a decision. You decide to move, despite the uncertainty. You act before you're fully confident. That's how confidence is built.

This is why discipline matters far more than motivation. Motivation is emotional. It comes and goes. But discipline is structural. It creates scaffolding that holds your goals even when life gets chaotic. And here's where habits are everything. Habits make execution automatic.

In The Power of Habit, Charles Duhigg explains the "habit loop," cue, routine, reward. Let's break this down through the lens of execution. Imagine your cue is your morning coffee. You attach a routine, writing 200 words, sketching your next prototype, or brainstorming business models. The reward? A sense of progress, momentum, or tracking a streak on a habit app. When this loop is repeated enough times, it becomes part of your identity. You're no longer just someone with ideas. You're someone who builds.

Yet, there is another enemy lurking in this process, perfectionism.

Perfectionism often masquerades as high standards, but it is really just fear dressed in fancy clothes. It convinces you not to launch until things are flawless. It whispers that it's better to plan than to risk looking unprepared. But the truth is, perfection is the enemy of progress. Most of the world's most successful companies started out messy, think Airbnb, which began with air mattresses on a floor, or Instagram, which pivoted completely from a failed app idea. The key wasn't perfection, It was iteration. Start before you're ready, Learn as you go.

This brings us to speed, not speed for speed's sake, but speed as a mindset. In a world that's evolving rapidly, the ability to move quickly is a competitive advantage. Jeff Bezos emphasized this with Amazon's philosophy of making decisions with 70 percent of the information, because waiting for certainty causes paralysis. Execution, then, is not about impulsivity. It's about refusing to let indecision choke opportunity.

Think about how many people stay stuck in planning mode forever. They map out color-coded strategies, buy courses, design logos, but they don't do the work. There's comfort in preparation because it avoids vulnerability. But the ones who succeed are not necessarily more talented. They simply shorten the gap between idea and action. Remember, the most important step is always the next one. Not the perfect one, Not the final one, Just the next one.

Let's explore a real-life example. Let's take, Elon Musk, a polarizing but undeniably prolific figure. Whether it's PayPal, SpaceX, or Tesla, what's consistent is his bias toward action. He's known for moving fast, breaking down ambitious visions into aggressive timelines, and shipping things when others are still debating whether it's possible. Musk's success is not rooted in ideas, but rather in executional courage. So how do you bring this home to your own life?

Start with an idea you've been sitting on. It could be a blog, a fitness journey, a YouTube channel, a workshop, or a side hustle. Write it down. Now ask yourself, What's the smallest next action I can take within the next 24 hours? Then ask, How can I build a daily habit around this?And finally, Who can I share this with to stay accountable?

You don't need to wait for inspiration to strike again. You don't need the perfect conditions. What you need is a plan, a process, and the willingness to do the work, especially when it's hard, lonely, or unclear. Let this be your wake-up call, The clock is ticking, not in a threatening way, but in a clarifying one. There's no perfect time to act, There is only now and only this step.

Execution is the difference between a life imagined and a life lived.

You weren't meant to be a dreamer who never finishes. You were meant to be a doer, someone who takes bold ideas and transforms them into impact. You were meant to leave behind a trail of finished projects, not abandoned plans. A legacy of contribution, not just contemplation.

So dream big, absolutely. But then move fast, whilst building the muscles of discipline. Shape the habits of action, because when you learn to bridge the gap between idea and execution, you stop being a passive observer of potential and become an active architect of your reality.

This is your moment. Don't just think it, do it.

Executing an idea successfully requires more than inspiration or a strong will. It demands a disciplined and structured approach that transitions a vision from abstract to actionable. Many great ideas never see the light of day, not because they lack potential, but because execution fails. The bridge between creativity and success is built with intentional strategy, relentless focus, and sustained effort. This process typically unfolds across four critical phases: planning, prototyping, testing, and iteration. Though simple in theory, mastering these stages requires clarity of purpose, mental resilience, and a deep understanding of how the human brain supports or resists execution.

Planning is the first and arguably most crucial phase. Without a clear plan, even the best ideas can spiral into chaos. Planning converts broad ambition into specific goals and structured tasks. It forces us to define what we want to achieve, why it matters, and how we intend to get there. A well-laid plan acts as a mental blueprint, providing direction, reducing uncertainty, and increasing focus. By breaking a large goal into smaller, achievable tasks, we make the journey more manageable. These micro-goals are easier to tackle and provide a consistent sense of progress. Techniques like setting SMART goals- goals that are Specific, Measurable, Achievable, Relevant, and Time-bound, are especially effective. They align your efforts with measurable benchmarks, reducing ambiguity and helping to maintain motivation.

Once a clear plan is in place, the next step is to move into prototyping. This stage is about execution without the need for perfection. Many people delay acting on an idea because they feel the conditions are not ideal, or the product isn't ready. Perfectionism kills momentum. A prototype helps you bypass this trap by focusing on creating a basic, functional version of your idea, what's known in startup culture as a Minimum Viable Product (MVP). Whether it's a draft of a book, a sketch of an app interface, or a sample marketing campaign, prototyping pushes your idea into the real world where it can be evaluated and refined. It's a courageous act that transforms mental energy into physical form. Importantly, it also helps build self-trust: the belief that you are capable of taking action despite uncertainty.

With a prototype ready, the third phase- testing, becomes the gateway to growth. Testing is not about proving that everything works perfectly. It's about collecting feedback, learning from results, and discovering what needs improvement. Feedback is information, not failure. The best ideas evolve through engagement with the real world. What people say, how they react, what resonates, and what doesn't, all these inputs guide the next version of your idea. Importantly, testing also helps to manage risk. By validating components of your idea on a small scale, you reduce the likelihood of costly mistakes during full implementation.

The final and ongoing stage is iteration. No idea, no matter how brilliant, is born perfect. Iteration is the process of improving, refining, and evolving your product, service, or system through repeated cycles. It's where resilience shows up, your ability to learn from setbacks, make changes, and keep moving forward. This stage differentiates those who persist from those who give up too soon. Through iteration, you build not just a better idea but a stronger version of yourself. It teaches adaptability, emotional regulation, and the value of feedback. Consistent, intelligent iteration is often the difference between good and great outcomes.

All of these stages are reinforced by the science of execution. The brain plays a central role in how we act or fail to act, in our intentions. The prefrontal cortex, the brain's executive center, governs decision-making, planning, and impulse control. However, this part of the brain requires significant mental energy and is vulnerable to fatigue. That's why your ability to execute tends to decrease over the course of the day. Willpower is not unlimited. To mitigate this, neuroscience recommends "front-loading" your day with your most important tasks. Research also supports the power of implementation intentions, clear if-then plans that tell your brain exactly what to do in specific situations. For instance, "If it's 8 AM, then I will write for 30 minutes." These pre-decisions reduce cognitive load and increase the likelihood of follow-through.

Dopamine, the brain's reward chemical, is another key player in execution. Dopamine is released when we experience novelty, progress, or achievement. It reinforces behavior and creates a positive feedback loop. Breaking your goal into micro-tasks and celebrating small wins keeps dopamine levels high and momentum steady. This is not about indulgence; it's about neuroscience. The brain craves completion, and every crossed-out item on your checklist feeds your desire to keep going.

Despite this structure and biological support, one powerful barrier often disrupts execution: procrastination. Procrastination is not just a time management issue. It's an emotional regulation issue. People procrastinate not because they don't know what to do, but because they don't want to feel what doing the task brings up. That might be fear of failure, fear of success, self-doubt, or even the discomfort of boredom. The brain interprets these emotions as threats and seeks to avoid them by diverting attention to more pleasurable activities. This is why you might find yourself scrolling social media or cleaning your desk instead of working on an important deadline.

From a psychological perspective, procrastination is rooted in what researchers call "present bias" or the tendency to prioritize immediate comfort over long-term rewards. This bias is compounded by "time inconsistency," which is the tendency of the human brain to value immediate rewards more highly than future ones. As a result, even if we logically understand that completing a task will benefit us in the long run, we may still avoid it because the discomfort is felt now, while the reward is distant.

Fortunately, procrastination is not a fixed trait. It can be managed and even overcome with intentional strategies. One of the most effective techniques is the five-minute rule. The idea is simple: commit to doing the task for just five minutes. The hardest part of any task is getting started, and once you begin, momentum usually kicks in. This small action helps bypass the mental resistance associated with large, overwhelming goals.

Another effective method is time blocking, where you schedule specific blocks of time for certain activities. Instead of waiting for motivation to strike, you rely on routine and structure. When the time arrives, you do the task, regardless of how you feel. This reduces decision fatigue and creates consistency. Research has shown that habits formed through repetition are more sustainable than those dependent on fluctuating willpower.

Environmental design also plays a significant role in execution. Your environment can either support your goals or sabotage them. Keeping your workspace clean, removing distractions, and having the tools you need within reach makes it easier to get started and stay focused. Even changing where you work can alter your mental state. For example, working in a quiet library versus a noisy café can dramatically affect your concentration.

Another useful tool is the Pomodoro Technique, where you work in focused intervals- typically 25 minutes- followed by a short five-minute break. This method capitalizes on the brain's natural attention span and makes long work sessions more manageable. It also creates a rhythm that supports productivity without burnout.

Accountability is another powerful motivator. When you declare your goals to someone else or commit publicly, you create external pressure that increases your chances of follow-through. Whether it's a coach, a colleague, or an accountability partner, having someone to check in with can transform your internal intentions into external results.

Finally, changing your self-identity is a deeper, more lasting strategy to beat procrastination. If you continually tell yourself, "I'm a procrastinator," your brain will look for ways to confirm that belief. Instead, shift your internal narrative to something empowering, like "I'm the kind of person who follows through." This small change can influence your decisions, behaviors, and long-term habits.

Execution is where the rubber meets the road. It's where ideas evolve into impact, and dreams turn into reality. It's often messy, uncomfortable, and filled with uncertainty, but it's also where growth happens. Mastering the art of execution means learning how to plan strategically, act decisively, and adapt continuously. It means understanding the science of your own brain and using that knowledge to create habits and systems that support action. And most importantly, it means facing procrastination with compassion, awareness, and practical tools that help you reclaim your time and potential.

The ability to execute well doesn't just build projects; it builds character. It trains your mind to delay gratification, embrace effort, and trust the process. In a world full of dreamers, the doers are the ones who make a difference. So the next time you feel overwhelmed by a big idea or paralyzed by resistance, remember that progress lies in starting small. One action. One prototype. One test. One revision. Keep going, and the gap between vision and reality will shrink until the two become indistinguishable. Execution is not an act of genius. It is an act of discipline and will and it's available to anyone willing to start.

Key notes from the chapter-

- Ideas don't change the world, execution does.
- Everyone has brilliant ideas. What sets creators, innovators, and leaders apart is the courage and consistency to act on them before they're "ready."
- Execution thrives on systems, not willpower.

- Habits, routines, and mental scaffolding- not occasional bursts of motivation, are what carry ideas across the finish line. You fall to the level of your systems.
- Perfectionism kills progress.
- Stop waiting to get it right. Start with what you have. Build messy. Iterate boldly. Movement, not mastery, is what brings clarity and momentum.
- Speed is a mindset, not a rush.
- Acting quickly shortens the distance between idea and impact. Don't wait for perfect conditions, decide, move, and adjust as you go.
- Procrastination is emotional, not logical.
- You're not lazy, you're avoiding discomfort. Use tools like the 5-minute rule, time blocking, and habit loops to bypass resistance and reclaim agency.
- Build identity, not just output.
- Execution isn't just about what you do,it's who you become. With every small action, you reinforce the belief: "I'm someone who follows through."

Conclusion

If you have made it this far towards the end of the book, I want you to give yourself a pat on the back. The discipline it takes to finish a book in the era of podcasts, short-form videos, and a dwindling attention span is quite commendable! But keeping the jest aside, I would like to emphasise for perhaps a hundredth time now, that no matter how much content you consume about reaching your highest self, all goes in vain unless you are actually manifesting the tips and tricks in your real life, incorporating the minute details onto your daily routine and making the most out of your comprehension of this book. Most of the chapters cover only about the tip of the iceberg on self actualization, the depth lies in your lived experience and in attempting, failing, and trying again.

Writing this book wasn't about pretending I have everything figured out. I don't. I'm still learning, growing, slipping up and getting back up. But I've learned enough to know that real change begins when we stop running from ourselves and start listening.

You don't need to burn yourself out chasing success, or force positivity when you're hurting, or wait for some perfect moment to begin. Everything starts with a quiet decision, 'I want better'. I'm ready for more. And maybe, for the first time in a long time, you're starting to believe that it's actually possible.

Throughout this book, we've talked about healing from the inside out, About rewiring your mind, prioritizing habits and routine, aligning with your values, and breaking free from patterns that aren't really yours and much more. And

I hope you felt seen, not judged or "fixed," but understood. This journey is less about becoming someone new, and more about remembering who you are before fear, shame, self-doubt, and comparison dimmed your light. You've always had the strength. You just needed tools, perspective, and a little bit of permission to trust yourself again. At its heart, this journey is about self-actualization and self-improvement: the lifelong process of growing into the fullest expression of who you are capable of becoming.

You don't need to do it all at once. You don't need a perfect plan. Just take the next right step. And then the next. Stay consistent, stay kind to yourself, and be patient with the process. There will be hard days. There will be setbacks. But none of that means you've failed. It means you're human.

And a very human urge we all have, is to go all in once we have finished reading a piece which might have inspired us. that is your emotion fuelling you, and emotions are fleeting, temporary and inconsistent. However, the key to building long-term success and gratifying life is, one must learn not to rely on a spur of motivation or inspiration, but on discipline and consistency, or showing up even on your toughest days. However, whenever you have an ample supply of inspiration, use it to its maximum when it comes by, As discussed in chapter 3, focus, fly and flow. Harnessing the creative flow is useful for a myriad of reasons.

Dont chase a perfect plan, just work towards your next step, and then the next. Stay consistent, stay kind to yourself, and be patient with the process.

So as you close this book, I hope you walk away with more than information. I hope you walk away with clarity. With a new kind of quiet confidence that says, "I've got this." Because you do. This book acts as a blueprint for success, drawing in from multiple real-life case studies on some of the most prominent and remarkable figures and on science-backed research, use it as a stepping tool to fulfill your true potential.

This isn't the end. It's just your next beginning. Take what you've learned. Use what resonates. Leave the rest. But whatever you do, don't stop showing up for yourself. You're closer than you think.

This book ends here, but your journey doesn't. Keep learning, healing and stay aligned, prioritize consistent imperfect action over motivation fuelled inconsistent actions. And when life gets heavy, return to this book, you might find a thing or two which might help get you back on track!

Endnotes

Chapter 1:

1. National Institute of General Medical Sciences. Circadian Rhythms Overview. https://www.nigms.nih.gov/education/fact-sheets/Pages/circadian-rhythms.aspx

2. Harvard Health Publishing. Blue Light Has a Dark Side. https://www.health.harvard.edu/staying-healthy/blue-light-has-a-dark-side

3. Cajochen, C. (2007). Alerting effects of light. *Sleep Medicine Reviews*, 11(6), 453–464. https://doi.org/10.1016/j.smrv.2007.07.009

4. Harvard Medical School. Waking up early may reduce depression risk. https://www.health.harvard.edu/mind-and-mood/waking-up-early-may-reduce-depression-risk

5. Daghlas, I., et al. (2021). Sleep Timing, Genetic Determinants, and Depression Risk. *JAMA Psychiatry*. https://jamanetwork.com/journals/jamapsychiatry/fullarticle/2780832

6. Scientific American. How Sunlight Can Influence Your Mood. https://www.scientificamerican.com/article/how-sunlight-can-influence-your-mood/

7. National Institute of Mental Health. Seasonal Affective Disorder. https://www.nimh.nih.gov/health/topics/seasonal-affective-disorder

8. American Psychological Association. The Exercise Effect. https://www.apa.org/monitor/2011/12/exercise

9. Harvard Health Publishing. Regular Exercise Changes the Brain. https://www.health.harvard.edu/mind-and-mood/regular-exercise-changes-the-brain-to-improve-memory-thinking

10. Sharma, R. *The 5 AM Club: Own Your Morning. Elevate Your Life.* HarperCollins. https://www.robinsharma.com/book/the-5am-club

11. Vanderkam, L. *What the Most Successful People Do Before Breakfast.* Portfolio Penguin. https://lauravanderkam.com/books/what-the-most-successful-people-do-before-breakfast/

12. National Sleep Foundation. Sleep and Cognition. https://www.sleepfoundation.org/how-sleep-works/sleep-and-cognition

13. National Heart, Lung, and Blood Institute. Why Is Sleep Important? https://www.nhlbi.nih.gov/health/sleep/why-sleep-important

14. Sleep Foundation. Caffeine and Sleep. https://www.sleepfoundation.org/nutrition/caffeine-and-sleep

15. Clark, I., & Landolt, H. P. (2017). Coffee, Caffeine, and Sleep: A Systematic Review. *Sleep Medicine Reviews.* https://doi.org/10.1016/j.smrv.2017.11.002

Chapter 2:

1. American Psychological Association. Mentorship Definition. https://dictionary.apa.org/mentoring
2. Harvard Business Review. What the Best Mentors Do. https://hbr.org/2019/02/what-the-best-mentors-do
3. Forbes. Why Every Person Needs a Mentor. https://www.forbes.com/sites/theyec/2019/07/15/why-every-person-needs-a-mentor/
4. National Mentoring Resource Center. What is Mentoring? https://nationalmentoringresourcecenter.org/index.php/what-is-mentoring.html
5. World Athletics. Usain Bolt Profile. https://worldathletics.org/athletes/jamaica/usain-bolt-14201817
6. The Guardian. Glen Mills: The Coach Behind Usain Bolt's Success. https://www.theguardian.com/sport/2009/aug/20/glen-mills-usain-bolt-coach
7. BBC Sport. Bolt Pays Tribute to Coach Mills. http://news.bbc.co.uk/sport2/hi/athletics/8180843.stm
8. *The Mahabharata*, Book 1. Sacred Texts. https://www.sacred-texts.com/hin/m01/m01134.htm
9. Encyclopaedia Britannica. Ekalavya. https://www.britannica.com/topic/Ekalavya
10. The New York Times. Google's New Chief and Founders.

https://www.nytimes.com/2011/01/21/technology/21google.html

11. Business Insider. How Eric Schmidt Mentored Google's Founders. https://www.businessinsider.com/how-eric-schmidt-helped-larry-page-and-sergey-brin-grow-up-2011-4

12. Fortune. Google's Management Evolution. https://fortune.com/2014/09/04/google-founders-management-style/

13. Harvard Business Review. Microsoft's Nadella Rewrites the Culture. https://hbr.org/2017/09/microsofts-ceo-on-how-to-build-a-learning-culture

14. Wired. Nadella's Cloud Strategy. https://www.wired.com/story/satya-nadella-rewrites-microsofts-code/

15. Fortune. How Tim Cook Stepped Out of Steve Jobs' Shadow. https://fortune.com/longform/apple-tim-cook-steve-jobs/

16. *Bhagavad Gita.* Full Text and Translation. https://www.sacred-texts.com/hin/gita/index.htm

Chapter 3:

1. Csikszentmihalyi, M. *Flow: The Psychology of Optimal Experience.* HarperCollins. https://www.harpercollins.com/products/flow-mihaly-csikszentmihalyi

2. TED Talk. Flow, the Secret to Happiness. https://www.ted.com/talks/mihaly_csikszentmihalyi_flow_the_secret_to_happiness

3. American Psychological Association. Flow Definition. https://dictionary.apa.org/flow

4. Positive Psychology. What is Flow in Psychology? https://positivepsychology.com/what-is-flow/

5. Harvard Business Review. The State of Flow. https://hbr.org/2014/03/creating-the-best-work-environment

6. Van Gogh Museum Amsterdam. https://www.vangoghmuseum.nl/en/art-and-stories/art/vincent-van-gogh

7. Biography.com. Vincent van Gogh Biography. https://www.biography.com/artists/vincent-van-gogh

8. Cameron, J. *James Cameron Biography.* https://www.biography.com/movies-tv/james-cameron

9. Variety. James Cameron on Making Avatar. https://variety.com/2022/film/news/james-cameron-avatar-making-of-1235431555/

10. Schwarzenegger, A. *Be Useful: Seven Tools for Life.* Penguin Random House. https://www.penguinrandomhouse.com/books/735498/be-useful-by-arnold-schwarzenegger/

11. Duhigg, C. *The Power of Habit.* https://charlesduhigg.com/the-power-of-habit/

12. Huberman Lab. Neuroplasticity Research. https://www.hubermanlab.com/episode/how-to-rewire-your-brain-with-dr-andrew-huberman

13. Naval Ravikant. *The Almanack of Naval Ravikant.* https://www.navalmanack.com/

14. Newport, C. *Deep Work.* https://www.calnewport.com/books/deep-work/

Chapter 4:

1. Harvard Business Review. *Creating a Purpose-Driven Organization.*
2. https://hbr.org/2018/07/creating-a-purpose-driven-organization
3. Forbes. *The Importance of Purpose in Business.*
4. https://www.forbes.com/sites/forbescoachescouncil/2018/07/19/the-importance-of-purpose-in-business/
5. Covey, S. R. *The 7 Habits of Highly Effective People.* Simon & Schuster, 1989.
6. https://www.franklincovey.com/the-7-habits/
7. Psychology Today. *Does Vision Boarding Really Help?*
8. https://www.psychologytoday.com/us/blog/the-moment-youth/201704/does-vision-boarding-really-help
9. Lifehack. *Why Vision Boards Work and How to Make One.*
10. https://www.lifehack.org/articles/productivity/why-vision-boards-work-and-how-to-make-one.html
11. Goleman, D. *Emotional Intelligence: Why It Can Matter More Than IQ.* Bantam, 1995.
12. https://www.danielgoleman.info/topics/emotional-intelligence/
13. Huberman Lab. *How to Set and Achieve Your Goals.*

14. https://www.hubermanlab.com/episode/how-to-set-and-achieve-your-goals

Chapter 5:

1. Dweck, C. S. *Mindset: The New Psychology of Success.* Random House, 2006.
2. https://www.mindsetworks.com/
3. Duckworth, A. *Grit: The Power of Passion and Perseverance.* Scribner, 2016.
4. https://angeladuckworth.com/grit-book/
5. Harvard Business Review. *Building Resilience.*
6. https://hbr.org/2011/04/building-resilience
7. American Psychological Association. *Building Your Resilience.*
8. https://www.apa.org/topics/resilience
9. Frankl, V. E. *Man's Search for Meaning.* Beacon Press, 2006.
10. https://www.beacon.org/Mans-Search-for-Meaning-P896.aspx
11. Harvard Health Publishing. *The Road to Resilience.*
12. https://www.health.harvard.edu/mind-and-mood/the-road-to-resilience

Chapter 6:

1. Newport, C. *Deep Work: Rules for Focused Success in a Distracted World.* Grand Central, 2016.
2. https://www.calnewport.com/books/deep-work/

3. Clear, J. *Atomic Habits: An Easy & Proven Way to Build Good Habits & Break Bad Ones.* Penguin, 2018.

4. https://jamesclear.com/atomic-habits

5. Pink, D. H. *When: The Scientific Secrets of Perfect Timing.* Riverhead Books, 2018.

6. https://www.danpink.com/books/when/

7. Scientific American. *How Your Chronotype Influences Your Day.*

8. https://www.scientificamerican.com/article/how-your-chronotype-influences-your-day/

9. American Psychological Association. *Why Wait? The Science Behind Procrastination.*

10. https://www.apa.org/news/press/releases/2010/04/procrastination

11. Huberman Lab. *Master Your Sleep and Be More Alert During the Day.*

12. https://www.hubermanlab.com/episode/master-your-sleep-and-be-more-alert-during-the-day

Chapter 7:

1. Kiyosaki, R. T. *Rich Dad Poor Dad.* Warner Books, 1997.

2. https://www.richdad.com/

3. Ravikant, N. *The Almanack of Naval Ravikant.*

4. https://www.navalmanack.com/

5. Forbes. *The Most Powerful Wealth-Building Strategy.*

6. https://www.forbes.com/sites/johnwasik/2014/03/04/the-most-powerful-wealth-building-strategy/
7. CNBC Make It. *Millionaire Habits That Anyone Can Adopt.*
8. https://www.cnbc.com/make-it/
9. Entrepreneur. *How to Build Multiple Income Streams.*
10. https://www.entrepreneur.com/money-finance/how-to-build-multiple-income-streams/439212
11. Investopedia. *Leverage Definition.*
12. https://www.investopedia.com/terms/l/leverage.asp

Chapter 8:

1. Dispenza, J. *Breaking the Habit of Being Yourself.* Hay House, 2012.
2. https://drjoedispenza.com/products/breaking-the-habit-of-being-yourself
3. Huberman Lab. *How to Rewire Your Brain.*
4. https://www.hubermanlab.com/episode/how-to-rewire-your-brain-with-dr-andrew-huberman
5. Goleman, D. *Emotional Intelligence.*
6. https://www.danielgoleman.info/topics/emotional-intelligence/
7. American Psychological Association. *Neuroplasticity.*
8. https://www.apa.org/monitor/2012/03/neuroplasticity
9. National Institute of Neurological Disorders and Stroke. *Brain Basics: Neuroplasticity.*

10. https://www.ninds.nih.gov/health-information/public-education/brain-basics/brain-basics-neuroplasticity

Chapter 9:

1. Frankl, V. E. *Man's Search for Meaning.*
2. https://www.beacon.org/Mans-Search-for-Meaning-P896.aspx
3. Dweck, C. S. *Mindset.*
4. https://www.mindsetworks.com/
5. Duckworth, A. *Grit.*
6. https://angeladuckworth.com/grit-book/
7. Taleb, N. N. *Antifragile: Things That Gain from Disorder.* Random House, 2012.
8. https://www.penguinrandomhouse.com/books/311076/antifragile-by-nassim-nicholas-taleb/
9. Harvard Business Review. *Building Resilience.*
10. https://hbr.org/2011/04/building-resilience

Chapter 10:

1. Dispenza, J. *Becoming Supernatural.* Hay House, 2017.
2. https://drjoedispenza.com/products/becoming-supernatural
3. National Center for Complementary and Integrative Health (NCCIH). *Meditation and Mindfulness.*
4. https://www.nccih.nih.gov/health/meditation-in-depth

5. International Center for Reiki Training. *What is Reiki?*

6. https://www.reiki.org/faqs/what-reiki

7. Harvard Health Publishing. *Meditation for Healthy Living.*

8. https://www.health.harvard.edu/mind-and-mood/meditation-for-healthy-living

Chapter 11:

1. Harvard Health Publishing. *Giving Thanks Can Make You Happier.*

2. https://www.health.harvard.edu/healthbeat/giving-thanks-can-make-you-happier

3. Emmons, R. A. *Thanks!: How the New Science of Gratitude Can Make You Happier.* Houghton Mifflin Harcourt, 2007.

4. https://greatergood.berkeley.edu/profile/robert_emmons

5. Psychology Today. *Gratitude.*

6. https://www.psychologytoday.com/us/basics/gratitude

7. Chopra, D. *The Seven Spiritual Laws of Success.* Amber-Allen Publishing, 1994.

8. https://chopra.com/articles/the-seven-spiritual-laws-of-success

Chapter 12: Sustaining Transformation

1. Huberman Lab. *How to Build Enduring Habits.*
2. https://www.hubermanlab.com/episode/how-to-build-enduring-habits
3. Clear, J. *Atomic Habits.*
4. https://jamesclear.com/atomic-habits
5. Dispenza, J. *Breaking the Habit of Being Yourself.*
6. https://drjoedispenza.com/products/breaking-the-habit-of-being-yourself
7. Duhigg, C. *The Power of Habit.* Random House, 2012.
8. https://charlesduhigg.com/the-power-of-habit/

Glossary

Chapter 1:

1. Circadian Rhythm *(noun)*
2. A natural internal process regulating the sleep–wake cycle over approximately 24 hours.
3. Melatonin *(noun)*
4. A hormone produced by the pineal gland that regulates sleep and wakefulness.
5. Anthropocene *(noun)*
6. The current geological epoch during which human activity has become the dominant influence on climate and environment.
7. Blue Light *(noun)*
8. High-energy visible light- often from screens and LEDs, suppresses melatonin and disrupts sleep.
9. Lifestyle Diseases *(noun)*
10. Health conditions (e.g. obesity, diabetes, cardiovascular issues) associated with poor diet, inactivity, and chronic stress.
11. Sleep Hygiene *(noun)*
12. Practices and habits that promote consistent, high-quality, and uninterrupted sleep.

Chapter 2:

1. Individualism
2. The principle of being independent and self-reliant, favoring individual freedom over collective control.
3. Subsystems
4. Independent components of a larger system that serve a shared function.
5. Circumnavigate *(figurative verb)*
6. To avoid an obstacle by using cunning strategy or indirect methods.
7. Self-actualization *(Psychology)*
8. The fulfillment of one's potential and talents, often depicted as the summit of human growth.
9. Kinship
10. A sense of connectedness or shared values beyond biological ties.
11. Psychosocial *(adjective)*
12. Relating to how psychological and social factors interact to shape development and behavior.
13. Rapport
14. A harmonious understanding or connection between individuals facilitating effective communication.

Chapter 3:

1. Flow
2. A mental state of full immersion where actions unfold intuitively and time perception changes.
3. Neuroplasticity
4. The brain's capacity to reorganize neural connections in response to experience.
5. Cognitive Absorption
6. Deep mental immersion that diminishes awareness of time and surroundings.
7. Intrinsic Motivation
8. The drive to act based on internal satisfaction, not external rewards.
9. Altered Time Perception
10. A distortion in sensing time's passage often occurs during flow states.
11. Optimal Experience
12. An activity that maximizes engagement, growth, and satisfaction.

Chapter 4:

1. Trauma
2. *noun*
3. A deeply distressing or disturbing experience, often with lasting emotional, psychological, or physiological effects.
4. Healing

5. *noun*

6. The process of restoring health, wholeness, or well-being, particularly after emotional or psychological injury.

7. Nervous System Regulation

8. *noun*

9. The ability of the autonomic nervous system to maintain balance between states of arousal (sympathetic) and calm (parasympathetic), often disrupted by trauma or chronic stress.

10. Inner Child

11. *noun*

12. A psychological concept referring to the childlike aspect within one's subconscious that holds emotional memories and unmet needs from early development.

13. Emotional Suppression

14. *noun*

15. The conscious or unconscious inhibition of emotional expression, often adopted as a coping mechanism to avoid vulnerability or pain.

16. Repression

17. *noun*

18. A defence mechanism whereby distressing thoughts, memories, or desires are excluded from conscious awareness.

19. Trigger

20. *noun*

21. A stimulus (such as a situation, sound, or smell) that elicits a strong emotional response, often linked to unresolved trauma.

22. Somatic Memory

23. *noun*

24. The body's physical memory of traumatic experiences, stored non-verbally and often expressed through tension, pain, or movement patterns.

25. Integration

26. *noun*

27. In a psychological context, the process of bringing together fragmented parts of the self, such as emotions, memories, and identities, into a cohesive whole.

28. Inner Safety

29. *noun*

30. A felt sense of security and stability within one's self, cultivated through practices that calm the nervous system and promote self-trust.

31. Hypervigilance

32. *noun*

33. A heightened state of sensory sensitivity and alertness, often associated with post-traumatic stress or anxiety disorders.

34. Dissociation

35. *noun*

36. A mental process of disconnecting from one's thoughts, feelings, memories, or sense of identity, commonly triggered by trauma.

37. Self-Compassion

38. noun

39. The practice of being kind, understanding, and nonjudgmental toward oneself, particularly in times of pain or failure.

40. Emotional Resilience

41. noun

42. The capacity to recover quickly from emotional difficulties and adapt to stress or adversity with flexibility and strength.

43. Energy Healing

44. noun

45. A holistic practice involving the channeling of healing energy into a person's body to balance physical, emotional, or spiritual health.

46. Grounding

47. noun

48. A therapeutic technique used to connect an individual to the present moment, often through sensory awareness or physical movement.

49. Catharsis

50. noun

51. The process of releasing, and thereby providing relief from, strong or repressed emotions.

52. Shadow Work

53. noun

54. A psychological and spiritual practice that involves exploring and integrating the unconscious or rejected aspects of the self.

55. Somatic Healing

56. *noun*

57. A body-centered approach to healing trauma, focusing on internal physical perception and the release of stored tension.

58. Mind-Body Connection

59. *noun*

60. The complex interaction between a person's mental and emotional processes and their physical state, recognizing their mutual influence on health.

Chapter 5:

1. Basal Ganglia

   Brain structures critical to habit formation and movement coordination.

2. Cue-Routine-Reward Loop

   A habit-formation cycle: a cue triggers a routine, reinforced by a reward.

3. Willpower (Ego-Depletion)

   The finite ability to resist impulses; mental fatigue can weaken self-control.

4. Synaptic Plasticity

   Changes in the strength of synaptic connections, underlying learning and habit formation.

5. Environment Design

   Structuring spaces or contexts to support desired behaviors and reduce friction.

6. Gut-Brain Axis

   The communication network linking gut microbiota and brain function, influencing mood and cognition.

7. Growth Mindset

   The belief that intelligence and abilities can develop through effort and learning.

8. Deliberate Practice

   Highly structured training aimed at improving performance through targeted feedback and effort.

9. Decision Fatigue

   Reduced decision quality after prolonged cognitive exertion.

10. Sleep Consolidation

    The neurological process of stabilizing memories during sleep for long-term retention.

Chapter 6:

1. Somatic Awareness

   Mind-body attunement that allows release of stored emotional or traumatic patterns.

2. Energetic Imprint

   Subtle energy residue from past emotional experiences believed to affect present behavior.

3. Inner Child Work

   Therapeutic practice addressing unmet childhood needs for emotional healing.

4. Emotional Transmutation

   Transforming negative emotions into higher-state consciousness or wisdom.

5. Limiting Beliefs

   Deeply held convictions that constrain potential and motivated action.

6. Energetic Blockage

   Disruptions in subtle lifeforce energy flow, often due to emotional or traumatic conditions.

7. Radical Acceptance

   Full acknowledgment of one's reality without resistance or judgment.

8. Integrative Healing

   A holistic wellness approach combining emotional, mental, physical, and spiritual modalities.

9. Energetic Sovereignty

   The ability to protect and govern one's emotional-energetic boundaries.

10. Psychospiritual Healing

    An integrated healing process addressing both psychological and spiritual dimensions.

11. Reparenting

    A self-healing practice offering oneself the care and nurturing missed in childhood.

61. Emotional Bypassing

Avoiding genuine emotion under the guise of positivity or spirituality.

62. Chakra Realignment

Rebalancing the body's energy centers (chakras) to promote well-being.

63. Soul Retrieval

A shamanic process of reclaiming fragmented aspects of the spirit lost to trauma.

Chapter 7:

1. Manifestation

The process of bringing intentions or desires into reality through belief, emotion, and aligned action.

2. Visualization

A cognitive technique involving vivid mental imagery of desired outcomes to build motivation.

3. Energetic Alignment

Harmony between thoughts, emotions, and behaviors aligned with one's intentions.

4. Reiki

A Japanese energy-healing method using hands-on or near-body channeling for wellbeing.

5. Life Force Energy

The vital energy (Prana, Qi) that flows through all living systems.

6. Mirror Work

   A self-affirmation technique using positive statements while facing oneself in a mirror.

7. Neural Pathways

   Chains of connected neurons; repetition solidifies thoughts or behaviors.

8. Scripting (journaling)

   Writing as if future goals are already realized to induce psychological immersion.

9. Subconscious Mind

   The part of the mind operating beneath awareness, influencing beliefs and behaviors.

10. Inspired Action

    Taking intuitive steps guided by inner knowing rather than deliberate planning.

11. Vibrational Frequency

    The quality or energy one emits spiritually or emotionally, thought to influence attraction.

12. Coherence (Energetic)

    Alignment of heart, mind, and body producing emotional and physiological balance.

13. Cognitive Reframing

    Changing perspective to replace limiting thoughts with constructive alternatives.

14. Empirical Evidence

    Information acquired through observation or experiment rather than theory.

15. Best Possible Self Exercise

    A practice of envisioning and writing about an ideal future self to enhance optimism.

16. Placebo Effect

    A positive outcome arising from belief or expectation, not active intervention.

Chapter 8:

(All chapter-8 terms already defined above; none repeated.)

Chapter 9:

1. Trauma

   Deeply distressing experiences that significantly alter mental, emotional, or physical states.

2. Nervous System Dysregulation

   A chronic imbalance in autonomic responses (fight/flight/freeze/fawn) due to trauma.

3. Energy Body / Energetic Imprint *(Term already defined; appears here for context.)*

   Inner Child *(Also defined above.)*

   Somatic Healing *(Also defined above.)*

4. Safe Space

   An environment; physical or emotional, where vulnerability is accepted without judgment.

5. Nervous System Regulation

   Techniques that restore balance and promote calm in trauma-impacted individuals.

6. Inner Dialogue / Self-Talk

   The internal conversation influencing self-worth and emotional resilience.

7. Coping Mechanisms

   Behaviors originally developed for survival that may limit growth if persistent.

8. Emotional Resilience

   The capacity to adapt and bounce back from adversity with flexibility and well-being.

9. Energetic Boundaries

   Invisible energy limits protecting emotional and personal integrity.

10. Inner Safety

    A felt sense of security rooted within, independent of external conditions.

11. Autonomic Nervous System (ANS)

    The involuntary system controlling bodily functions and emotional responses.

12. Fight, Flight, Freeze, Fawn

    Four instinctive survival modes activated by trauma or threat.

13. Hypervigilance

    Excessive alertness to perceived threats, typically associated with trauma history.

14. Grounding Techniques

    Simple practices (e.g. breathwork, sensory awareness) that anchor attention to the present.

15. Dissociation

    A psychological detachment from moment-to-moment experience, often as a coping response.

16. Pattern Recognition (in Healing)

    The awareness of recurring emotional cycles or behaviors rooted in past wounds.

Chapter 10:

(Chapter-10 defines many terms already listed; no new unique terms beyond those above.)

Chapter 11:

1. Artificial Intelligence (AI)

   Systems or machines that simulate human intelligence, learning, and decision-making.

2. Chronotype

   An individual's intrinsic biological rhythm influencing peak alertness and productivity timings.

3. Time Blocking

   A productivity method assigning specific time periods for particular tasks or focus.

4. BMC Psychology

   A peer-reviewed journal publishing longitudinal and experimental psychological research.

5. 100. Two-Minute Rule

   A productivity strategy: act immediately on any task that takes less than two minutes.

6. Momentum (behavioral science)

   The psychological reinforcement loop where small wins fuel continued action.

7. Self-Compassion

   Treating oneself with kindness and understanding during difficulty or failure.

Chapter 12:

1. Ideation- The capacity for or the act of forming or entertaining ideas.

2. Identity-based Habit -

   Identity-based habits are actions that stem from a desired self-image, rather than focusing solely on achieving specific outcomes.

3. Present Bias / Time Inconsistency -

   Present bias, also known as time inconsistency, describes the human tendency to overvalue immediate rewards while undervaluing future benefits.